First World War
and Army of Occupation
War Diary
France, Belgium and Germany

50 DIVISION
Divisional Troops
Durham Light Infantry
1/7th Battalion Pioneers
1 December 1915 - 30 June 1918

WO95/2823/2

The Naval & Military Press Ltd
www.nmarchive.com
Published in association with The National Archives

Published by

The Naval & Military Press Ltd

Unit 10 Ridgewood Industrial Park,

Uckfield, East Sussex,

TN22 5QE England

Tel: +44 (0) 1825 749494

www.naval-military-press.com

www.nmarchive.com

This diary has been reprinted in facsimile from the original. Any imperfections are inevitably reproduced and the quality may fall short of modern type and cartographic standards.

© Crown Copyright
Images reproduced by permission of The National Archives, London, England, 2015.

Contents

Document type	Place/Title	Date From	Date To
Heading	WO95/2823 So Div 1/7 Durham L.I. (Pioneers) Dec15-Jun 18		
Heading	1-7th Bn Durham Lt Infy. (Pioneers) Dec 1915-Jun 1918		
Heading	1/7th Durham L. I. Dec Vol VIII		
War Diary	Bailleul	01/12/1915	16/12/1915
War Diary	Dicke Busch	17/12/1915	31/12/1915
Heading	1/7 Durham L. I. Jan Vol IX		
War Diary	Dickebusch	01/01/1916	29/02/1916
Heading	1/7 Durham L. I. Vol XI		
War Diary	Dickebusch	01/03/1916	04/04/1916
War Diary	Scherpenberg	05/04/1916	25/04/1916
War Diary	La. Clytte	26/04/1916	03/05/1916
War Diary	Meteren Area	04/05/1916	06/05/1916
War Diary	Meteren	07/05/1916	19/05/1916
War Diary	La Clytte	20/05/1916	23/05/1916
War Diary	Scherpenberg	24/05/1916	30/06/1916
Heading	War Diary 7th Battalion (Pioneers) Durham Light Infantry July. 1916 Volume No 15		
War Diary	Scherpenberg	01/07/1916	31/07/1916
Miscellaneous	Operation Orders		
Heading	War Diary Of 7th Battn. Durham Light Infantry (Pioneers) Volume XVII From 1st to 31st August, 1916 vol 16		
War Diary	Scherpenberg	01/08/1916	06/08/1916
War Diary	Fletre	07/08/1916	11/08/1916
War Diary	Berneuil	12/08/1916	15/08/1916
War Diary	Vignacourt	16/08/1916	16/08/1916
War Diary	Pierregot	17/08/1916	17/08/1916
War Diary	Baizieux	18/08/1916	31/08/1916
Heading	7th. Durham Light Infantry (Pioneers) 50th. Division September 1916		
Miscellaneous	Officers Charges will accompany the Transport		
Heading	War Diary. Of 7th Battalion (Pioneers) Durham Light Infantry. September, 1916 Volume No		
War Diary	Baizieux	01/09/1916	03/09/1916
War Diary	Becourt	04/09/1916	13/09/1916
War Diary	Fricourt	14/09/1916	30/09/1916
Operation(al) Order(s)	Operation Order No.2		
Map			
Heading	War Diary Of 7th Battalion D.L.I (Pioneers)		
War Diary	Fricourt	01/10/1916	13/10/1916
Miscellaneous	1/7 Durham L I Vol XII		
War Diary	Fricourt	13/10/1916	24/10/1916
War Diary	Mametz	25/10/1916	31/10/1916
Operation(al) Order(s)	50th Division Operation Order Number 55	21/09/1916	21/09/1916
Heading	War Diary 1/7th Battalion Durham Light Infantry 1st-30th November 1916		
Heading	War Diary Of 7th D.L.I. (Pioneers).		
War Diary	Mametz	01/11/1916	30/11/1916

Operation(al) Order(s)	50th Division Operation Order No. 62	03/11/1916	03/11/1916
Operation(al) Order(s)	Re 50th Division O.O. No. 60	31/10/1916	31/10/1916
Operation(al) Order(s)	50th Division Operation Order No. 60	26/10/1916	26/10/1916
Operation(al) Order(s)	50th Division O.O. No 60 Para 4	31/10/1916	31/10/1916
Heading	War Diary Of 7th Battalion Durham Light Infantry (Pioneers).		
War Diary	Mametz	01/12/1916	31/12/1916
Miscellaneous	Herewith Extract From 50th Div/G.X. 3155	26/12/1916	26/12/1916
Map	50th Division Trench Map		
Miscellaneous	Belloy Sector		
Map			
Miscellaneous	Belloy Sector		
Heading	War Diary Of 7th Battalion D.L.I. (Pioneers). Vol 21		
War Diary	Mametz	01/01/1917	31/01/1917
War Diary	Baizieux	01/02/1917	09/02/1917
War Diary	Hamel	10/02/1917	11/02/1917
War Diary	Bois St Martin	12/02/1917	28/02/1917
Heading	War Diary Of 7th Batt D.L.I. (Pioneers) Volumn XXIV		
War Diary	Bois St Martin	01/03/1917	08/03/1917
War Diary	Morcourt	09/03/1917	31/03/1917
Operation(al) Order(s)	7th Bn Durham L.I. Pioneers Operation Orders No. 8	02/03/1917	02/03/1917
Operation(al) Order(s)	Operation Order No. 1		
Operation(al) Order(s)	Operation Orders. No 3	12/03/1917	12/03/1917
Operation(al) Order(s)	7th Bn Durham L.I. Pioneers Operation Orders. No. 4	24/03/1917	24/03/1917
Operation(al) Order(s)	7th Durham Light Infantry Pioneers Operation Orders. No. 5	29/03/1917	29/03/1917
Operation(al) Order(s)	7th Bn. Durham Lt Infty Pioneers Operation Orders No. 6	30/03/1914	30/03/1914
War Diary	In The Field	01/04/1917	30/04/1917
Operation(al) Order(s)	7th Durham L.I Pioneers Operation Orders No. 7	01/04/1917	01/04/1917
Operation(al) Order(s)	7th Bn D.L.I Pioneers. Operation Orders No 9	03/04/1917	03/04/1917
Operation(al) Order(s)	7th Bn D.L.I. (Pioneers) Operation Orders No. 10	06/04/1917	06/04/1917
Operation(al) Order(s)	7th Bn Durham Light Infantry Pioneers Operation Orders No. 11	07/04/1917	07/04/1917
Operation(al) Order(s)	7th Bn Durham L I Pioneers Operation Orders No. 12	09/04/1917	09/04/1917
Operation(al) Order(s)	7th D.L.I (Pioneers) Operation Order No 13		
Miscellaneous	Addendum No 1 To Operation Order No. 13	27/04/1917	27/04/1917
Operation(al) Order(s)	7th Bn D.L.I (Pioneers) Operation Orders No 14	30/04/1917	30/04/1917
Heading	War Diary Of 7th Battalion Durham Light Infantry (Pioneers). Volume XXVI		
War Diary	In The Field	01/05/1917	31/05/1917
Operation(al) Order(s)	7th D.L.I (Pioneers) Operation Orders No 15	01/05/1917	01/05/1917
Operation(al) Order(s)	Operation Order No. 14	30/04/1917	30/04/1917
Operation(al) Order(s)	7th Bn Durham L.I (Pioneers) Operation Orders No 16	05/05/1917	05/05/1917
Miscellaneous	7th D.L.I. (Pioneers). Add To Operation Orders No 15	02/05/1917	02/05/1917
Miscellaneous	Movement Orders No 17	24/05/1917	24/05/1917
Operation(al) Order(s)	7th D.L.I. Pioneers Operation Orders No 18	29/05/1917	29/05/1917
Operation(al) Order(s)	7th Bn Durham L.I (Pioneers) Operation Orders No. 19	30/05/1917	30/05/1917
Heading	War Diary Of 7th Battalion, The Durham Light Infantry, (Pioneers) Vol 26		
War Diary	In The Field	01/06/1917	30/06/1917
Operation(al) Order(s)	Operation Orders No. 20	16/06/1917	16/06/1917
Miscellaneous	War Diary		
Heading	War Diary Of 7th Battalion, The Durham Light Infantry (Pioneers). Volume XXVIII July 1917		
War Diary	In The Field	01/07/1917	31/07/1917

Heading	War Diary Of 7th. B.N. Durham Light Infantry (Pioneers) Volume XXIX August 1917		
War Diary	In The Field	01/08/1917	31/08/1917
Heading	War Diary Of 7th. Battn. Durham Light Infantry. (Pioneers). Volume XXX. September 1917		
War Diary	In The Field	01/09/1917	30/09/1917
Heading	War Diary Of 7th. Bn. Durham Light Infantry (Pioneers). Volume XXXI.		
War Diary	In The Field	01/10/1917	30/10/1917
Miscellaneous	Transport Officer.	23/10/1917	23/10/1917
Operation(al) Order(s)	7th Bn. The Durham Light Infantry (Pioneers). Operation Order No. 24	23/10/1917	23/10/1917
Operation(al) Order(s)	7th Bn. The Durham Light Infantry Pioneers. Operation Order No. 25	28/10/1917	28/10/1917
Miscellaneous	The Following Alteration Are Made To Operation Order No 25	28/10/1917	28/10/1917
War Diary	In The Field	31/10/1917	31/10/1917
Operation(al) Order(s)	Operation Order No. 21	05/10/1917	05/10/1917
Operation(al) Order(s)	7th Bn. The Durham Light Infantry (Pioneers) Operation Order No. 28	16/10/1917	16/10/1917
Operation(al) Order(s)	Operation Order No. 23	20/10/1917	20/10/1917
Heading	War Diary Of 7th Battn. Durham Light Infantry (Pioneers). Volume XXXII. November 1917		
War Diary	Elverdinghe	01/11/1917	08/11/1917
War Diary	Hulls Farm	09/11/1917	30/11/1917
Miscellaneous	Table "A"		
Miscellaneous	To O.C. 7th D.L.I. Pioneer Battalion.		
Miscellaneous	7th Bn. Durham Light Infantry.	30/11/1917	30/11/1917
Operation(al) Order(s)	7th Bn. The Durham Light Infantry Pioneers. Operation Order No 24	30/11/1917	30/11/1917
Operation(al) Order(s)	7th Bn. The Durham Light Infantry Pioneers. Operation Orders No. 24	30/11/1917	30/11/1917
Heading	War Diary Of 7th Battalion Durham. L. Infy (Pioneers). Volume No XXXIII December 1917		
War Diary	In The Field	01/12/1917	31/12/1917
Operation(al) Order(s)	7th Bn. The Durham Light Infantry, Pioneers. Operation Order No. 26	10/12/1917	10/12/1917
Miscellaneous	7th D.L.I. (Pioneers)	11/12/1917	11/12/1917
Miscellaneous	Headquarters 50th Division.	14/12/1917	14/12/1917
Operation(al) Order(s)	7th Bn. The Durham Light Infantry Pioneers. Operation Order No. 27	11/12/1917	11/12/1917
Heading	War Diary Of 7th Battalion Durham Light Infantry (Pioneers). Volume XXXIV		
War Diary	In The Field	01/01/1918	31/01/1918
Miscellaneous	Transport Officer.	19/01/1918	19/01/1918
Miscellaneous	7th Bn. The Durham Light Infantry Pioneers.	20/01/1918	20/01/1918
Operation(al) Order(s)	7th Bn. The Durham Light Infantry Pioneers. Operation Order No. 28	20/01/1918	20/01/1918
Operation(al) Order(s)	7th Bn. The Durham Light Infantry Pioneers. Operation Order No. 29	26/01/1918	26/01/1918
Heading	War Diary Of 7th Battalion Durham Light Infantry (Pioneers) Volume XXXV.		
War Diary	In The Field	01/02/1918	28/02/1918
Operation(al) Order(s)	7th Bn. The Durham Light Infantry Pioneers. Operation Order No. 30	19/02/1918	19/02/1918
Miscellaneous	Table "A"		

Miscellaneous	7th Bn. The Durham Light Infantry Pioneers.	16/02/1918	16/02/1918
Heading	7th Battalion (Pioneers) Durham Light Infantry March 1918		
War Diary	Field	01/03/1918	31/03/1918
Miscellaneous	7th. Bn. The Durham Light Infantry, Pioneers.		
Miscellaneous	7th Bn. The Durham Light Infantry Pioneers. Warning Order.		
Operation(al) Order(s)	7th Bn. The Durham Light Infantry Pioneers. Operation Order No. 51.		
Operation(al) Order(s)	7th Bn. The Durham Light Infantry Pioneers. Operation Order No 32	10/02/1918	10/02/1918
Miscellaneous	7th Bn. The Durham Light Infantry Pioneers	15/03/1918	15/03/1918
Operation(al) Order(s)	7th Bn. The Durham Light Infantry Pioneers. Operation Order No 34	16/03/1918	16/03/1918
Miscellaneous	Instructions For More		
Operation(al) Order(s)	Operation Order No. 29		
Heading	1/7th Battalion Durham Light Infantry Pioneers April 1918		
Heading	War Diary Of 7th Bn. D.L.I. (Pioneers) For Month Of April 1918 Volume XXXVII		
War Diary	In The Field	01/04/1918	30/04/1918
Operation(al) Order(s)	7th Bn. The Durham Light Infantry Pioneers. Operation Orders. No 37	17/04/1918	17/04/1918
Operation(al) Order(s)	7th Bn. The Durham Light Infantry Pioneers. Operation Order No. 36	06/04/1918	06/04/1918
Operation(al) Order(s)	7th Bn. The Durham Light Infantry Pioneers. Operation Order No. 35	03/04/1918	03/04/1918
Operation(al) Order(s)	7th Bn. The Durham Light Infantry Pioneers. Operation Order No 38	25/04/1918	25/04/1918
Miscellaneous	7th Bn. Durham Light Infantry Pioneers Weekly Training Programme		
Heading	7th Bn Durham Light Infantry May & June 1918		
Heading	War Diary Of 7th Durham Light Infantry (Pioneers). Volume XXXVIII May, 1918		
War Diary	Field	01/05/1918	30/06/1918
Miscellaneous	8th Division		
Miscellaneous	Table A		
Operation(al) Order(s)	7th Durham L.I Infantry Operation Order No. 172	09/06/1918	09/06/1918
Operation(al) Order(s)	Operation Order No. 13	19/06/1918	19/06/1918

WO 95/2823
50 Div
1/7 Durham L.I. (Pioneers)
Dec '15 - Jun '18

(2)

50TH DIVISION

1-7TH BN DURHAM LT INFY.
(PIONEERS)
DEC 1915-JUN 1918

FROM 151 BDE 50 DIV

TO 8 DIV TROOPS

1/7i Sudan 1.1.
Sec
vol. VIII

D/
7957

117 D.L.Y.
32/
Army Form C. 2118.

WAR DIARY
INTELLIGENCE SUMMARY.

Dec. 1915

Place	Date	Hour	Summary of Events and Information	Remarks and references to Appendices
BAILLEUL	1st	—	In Billets as above.	MBR
"	2nd	—	The Battalion, less C Coy's, carried out a Route March of 12 miles.	CBK
"	3rd	—	In Billets as above.	
"	4th	—	C Coy rejoined the Battalion.	KBK
"	5th	—	The Battalion carried out a Route March of 12 miles	
"	6th	—	The Battalion practised the Attack on an Enemy System of trenches.	MK
"	7th	—	The Battalion carried out a Coy's attack of 14 miles.	
"	8th	—	A Coy. commenced today a field firing.	
"	9th	—	B Coy & D Coy practised the "Attack"; C and A Coys carried out Route Marches of 10 miles.	CBK
"	10th	—	A & B Companies fired Grouping practices on the 30 yards Range. The shooting was excellent.	
"	11th	—	C & D Companies fired Grouping practices on the 30yds Range. The shooting was also excellent.	CBK
"	12th	—	In Billets as above. Church Parades were held.	

Army Form C. 2118.

WAR DIARY
or
INTELLIGENCE SUMMARY.
(Erase heading not required.)

53.
Dec, 1915.

Place	Date	Hour	Summary of Events and Information	Remarks and references to Appendices
BAILLEUL	12th	—	In Billets as above.	NSR
"	14th	—	In Billets as above.	N.7.R.
"	15th	—	Sir Charles Fergusson said "Goodbye" to the Battalion and congratulated it on the fine work which it had done.	NSR
"	16th	—	In Billets as above.	N.7.R.
DICKEBUSCH	17th	—	H.Qrs & B Coy moved to CANADA HUTS near Dickebuch.	N.7.R.
"	18th	—	D Coy moved to CANADA HUTS.	N.7.R.
"	19th	—	C Coy moved to CANADA HUTS.	N.7.R.
"	20th	—	A Coy moved to CANADA HUTS.	N.7.R.
"	—	—	D Coy attached to 151st Brigade moved to YPRES	N.7.R.
"	21st	—	B Coy attached to 150th Brigade moved to RAILWAY DUG-OUTS.	N.7.R.
"	22nd	—	C Coy attached to 149th Brigade moved to BEDFORD HOUSE.	N.7.R.
"	—	—	B Coy moved to CANADA HUTS.	—
"	23rd	—	A Coy and B worked at CANADA HUTS.	N.7.R.
"	—	—	D Coy and C worked for respective Brigades	
"	24th	—	As above.	N.7.R.

Army Form C. 2118.

WAR DIARY
or
INTELLIGENCE SUMMARY.
(Erase heading not required.)

3 4

Dec. 1915.

Place	Date	Hour	Summary of Events and Information	Remarks and references to Appendices
DICKEBUSCH	25th	—	As above. Church Parades were held.	N.7.2.
"	26th	—	As above	N.7.2.
"	27th	—	A Coy moved to YPRES and relieved D Coy.	N.7.2.
"	—	—	B Coy attached to 150th Brigade moved to YPRES.	N.7.2.
"	28th	—	A, B and C Coys worked for respective Brigades	N.7.2.
"	—	—	D Coy worked at CANADA HUTS and DICKEBUSCH.	
"	29th	—	As above.	N.7.2.
"	30th	—	As above	N.7.2.
"	31st	—	As above	N.7.2.

1/4 Durham L. I.
Jan
Vol. IX

50

Army Form C. 2118.

35.

WAR DIARY
or
INTELLIGENCE SUMMARY.

(Erase heading not required.)

January 1916.

Place	Date	Hour	Summary of Events and Information	Remarks and references to Appendices
DICKEBUSCH hut	1st		A and B. Coys. remained in YPRES. A. Coy. was attached to the 150th. Brigade and B. Coy. to the 150th Brigade. C. Coy. remained at Bedford House and was attached to the 149th. Brigade. D. Coy. and Headquarters remained at CANADA HUTS.	RBB
"	2nd		As above	RBB
"	3rd		As above.	
"	4th		D. Coy. relieved C. Coy. at BEDFORD HOUSE.	RBB
"	5th		As above.	
"	6th		As above.	RBB
"	7th		As above.	
"	8th		As above.	RBB
"	9th		As above. The work in which the Companies (A - B - D) are engaged consists in getting communication trenches and making special dugouts for Machine Gunners.	
"	"		C.O. wrote letter to the G.O.C. 50th Brigade very heavily, saying that he was dissatisfied with the work done by	RBB

WAR DIARY
or
INTELLIGENCE SUMMARY.
(Erase heading not required.)

Army Form C. 2118.

36/

January 1916

Place	Date	Hour	Summary of Events and Information	Remarks and references to Appendices
DICKEBUSCH	10th	—	B Coy. relieved D Coy. at BEDFORD HOUSE.	RMcK
"	11th	—	As above.	
"	12th	—	As above. The Duke of Northumberland visited CANADA HUTS.	RMcK
"	13th	—	As above.	
"	14th	—	As above. The 3 Companies attacked to the Brigade were working about 8 hours a day.	
"	15th	—	The Duke of Northumberland again visited the HUTS (Canada Huts).	RMcK
"	16th	—	B Coy. relieved 1 Coy. 7th Platoon of B Coy. went up to SANCTUARY WOOD YPRES — attached to the 5th N.F. Brigade. Two Platoons of B Coy. they were required for constructing and stayed in dugouts. Three were required for constructing special dugouts in the front line trenches.	
"	18th	—	As above. Repair Workshop for Vehicles was started at CANADA HUTS under the direction of Capt. A.C. Mackintyre.	RMcK
"	19th	—	As above.	
"	20th	—	As above.	

WAR DIARY
INTELLIGENCE SUMMARY

Army Form C. 2118.

January 1916.

Place	Date	Hour	Summary of Events and Information	Remarks and references to Appendices
DICKEBUSCH.	21st.	—	As above. Work was commenced on a new Grande School (Divisional) in DICKEBUSCH CAMP.	
"	22nd.	—	As above. Ypres was shelled fairly heavily at about 3 p.m. as were mbr of R.E. Boys. were returning from work. No casualties however were suffered.	WD
"	23rd.	—	As above.	
"	24th.	—	A Coy. relieved B Coy. in Ypres — and became attached to the 15th. Infantry Brigade. Gl. Wilkinson visited CANADA & DICKEBUSCH HUTS.	RSB
"	25th.	—	As above. The work our Companies with the Brigades are doing now consists in revetting and draining communication trenches, and in making special strong dugouts.	RSB
"	26th.	—	As above. Work was commenced on a 30 yards Range in DICKEBUSCH CAMP.	
"	27th. 28th.	—	The Battalion remained disposed as above. A bicycle repairing depot was started under the direction of A/Q.	

Army Form C. 2118.

WAR DIARY
or
INTELLIGENCE SUMMARY.
(Erase heading not required.)

3.8 / Jan. 1916.

Place	Date	Hour	Summary of Events and Information	Remarks and references to Appendices
DICKEBUSCH	29th	—	M. St. Pryce — to repair bicycles for the Units of the Division. The Battalion rendered disposed by stove.	MB
"	30th	—	D Coy. relieves C Coy. at BEDFORD HOUSE.	MB
"	31st	—	The Grenade School in Rickebusch Camp was finished — 3 p.m. daily. The men are now working from 9 a.m.	MB

M.B. Bradford
Capt. & Adjt.
7. R. W.

Army Form C. 2118.

WAR DIARY
or
INTELLIGENCE SUMMARY.
(Erase heading not required.)

89/ February 1916.

Place	Date	Hour	Summary of Events and Information	Remarks and references to Appendices
DICKEBUSCH	1st.	—	The Battalion was disposed as above.	RBB
"	2nd.	—	The Battalion was disposed as above. Brig. Gen Clifford sent for Col Vaux to state that the Brigade (149th) Infantry to which he (Col Vaux) & B Coy (attached to his Brigade) had done excellent and valuable work. The work B Coy have been doing for the last three days has been mainly night work.	RBB
"	3rd.	—	Battalion disposed as above.	RBB
"	4th.	—	Battalion disposed as above. C Coy commenced work on making a 100 yards range in Dickebusch Camp.	
"	5th.	—	YPRES was heavily shelled intermittently throughout the day. Our two companies there were very fortunate to escape casualties.	RBB
"	6th.	—	Battalion disposed as above.	RBB
"	7th.	—	C Coy relieved B Coy. in YPRES B Coy returned to CANADA HUTS	RBB

Army Form C. 2118.

WAR DIARY
or
INTELLIGENCE SUMMARY.
(Erase heading not required.)

February 1916

Place	Date	Hour	Summary of Events and Information	Remarks and references to Appendices
DICKEBUSCH	8th	—	Battalion disposed as above	ARB
"	9th	—	Lieut. Gen. Plumer (5th Corps) inspected CANADA and DICKEBUSCH HUTS. He told Col. Saux that he was very pleased with the fine work which had been done by the 7th B.L.I. in making such excellent camps.	ARB
"	10th	—	The companies attached to the Brigades are now working intently by day — from 9 am — 3 pm daily.	ARB
"	11th	—	Battalion disposed as above.	
"	12th	—	Battalion disposed as above.	
"	13th	—	The Band played a programme in the Y.M.C.A. CANADA HUTS after Parade Services.	ARB
"	14th	—	The enemy shelled YPRES & SANCTUARY WOOD very heavily. We lost one man — Pte. Thwaites — killed and four wounded.	
"	"	"	The boys at BEDFORD HOUSE — D Coy. — is now working entirely by night. Their work consists in reclaiming old communication trenches and local communication trenches.	ARB

Army Form C. 2118.

WAR DIARY
or
INTELLIGENCE SUMMARY.

(Erase heading not required.)

February 1916.

Instructions regarding War Diaries and Intelligence Summaries are contained in F.S. Regs., Part II and the Staff Manual respectively. Title pages will be prepared in manuscript.

Place	Date	Hour	Summary of Events and Information	Remarks and references to Appendices
DICKEBUSCH HUTS	14th	—	B Coy. relieved A Coy — but moved to CANAL DUGOUTS instead of being billetted in YPRES.	MB
"	15th	—	The Battalion was disposed as above	CWB
"	16th	—	As above. A violent gale raged throughout the day. A Zeppelin passed over CANADA HUTS at midnight.	CWB
"	17th	—	As above	
"	18th	—	New item Totswell Coverd party — four in number made gave a splendid concert at the Y.M.C.A. Major Hunt took the chair.	WB
"	19th	—		
"	20th	—	The Battalion was disposed as above	
"	21st	—	A Company relieved D Coy. at BEDFORD HOUSE.	
"	22nd	—	A Party of 45 men under 2nd Lieut. E.J. Foster proceeded to EMINGHELST to practise making dummy assembly trenches to R.E. tracks with canvas.	CWB
"	23rd	—	A party of 20 men from D Coy. under 2nd Lieut. Balgiel made a Jadeine road in MOREBUSH CAMP.	WB

1577 Wt.W10791/1773 500,000 1/15 D. D. & L.   A.D.S.S./Forms/C. 2118.

Army Form C. 2118.

WAR DIARY
or
INTELLIGENCE SUMMARY.
(Erase heading not required.)

February 1916.

Place	Date	Hour	Summary of Events and Information	Remarks and references to Appendices
DICKEBUSCH	24th	—	The Party of 45 n.c.o. (D. Coy) under 2nd Lt. F.F. FORSTER proceeded to TRANSPORT FARM at 9 p.m. where they met Brig. Gen. J. SHEA who showed them where the dummy assembly trenches were to be made. The party made them quickly & well and received great praise from the Divisional	RBB
"	25th	—		RBB
"	24th	—		RBB
"	25th	—	An Aeroplane dropped two bombs on Dickebusch Camp. The Northwest Canadian Band played a programme at the Y.M.C.A.	RBB
"	26th	—	As above	RBB
"	27th	—	As above	RBB
"	28th	—	D Company relieved C Coy. in YPRES.	RBB
"	29th	—	A Party of fifty men from C Coy. under 2nd Lt. N. Abradlog went out from CANADA HUTS at 9 p.m. and worked on wiring the G.H.Q. 2nd line. The party returned at 4 a.m.	RBB

M. Bradage
Capt. & Adjt.
J.T.I.

50

1/7 Durham L.I.
Vol XI

Army Form C. 2118.

WAR DIARY
or
INTELLIGENCE SUMMARY.
(Erase heading not required.)

43.

March 1916

Place	Date	Hour	Summary of Events and Information	Remarks and references to Appendices
DICKEBUSCH	1st.	—	The Battalion was disposed as above.	RBB
"	2nd.	—	As above. The Band played a Programme in the Y.M.C.A. CANADA HUTS at 6 p.m.	RBB
"	3rd.	—	A Party of 100 men from C Coy under 2nd Lts W.C. Bradley & Dobson went up to Belford House at 9 p.m. and continued the work of wiring the G.H.Q. 2nd Line. The C.R.E. expressed great pleasure at the work which this Party carried out.	RBB
"	4th.	—	As above.	
"	5th.	—	A party of sixty men (30 from C Coy. & 30 from M.G. Detachment) under 2nd Lt. A. Bradley went up & continued the wiring of the G.H.Q. 2nd Line.	RBB
"	6th.	—	A Party of sixty men (30 from B Coy. & 30 from M.G. Detachment) under 2nd Lt. Bradley continued the wiring on the G.H.Q. 2nd Line. B Coy returned to YPRES - B Coy relieved by C Coy in CANADA HUTS.	RBB

WAR DIARY or INTELLIGENCE SUMMARY

Army Form C. 2118.

March 1916.

Place	Date	Hour	Summary of Events and Information	Remarks and references to Appendices
DICKEBUSCH	7th	—	A Party of Sixty men (30 from B Coy + 30 from M.G. Detachment) under 2nd Lt Bradley continued the work in the G.H.Q. 2nd Line.	RBB
"	"	—	The work the three Companies in the forward billets are doing at present consists of revetting the front line trenches, constructing Machine Gun Emplacements, Strong Dugouts in or near the front line, and improving the drainage system of the front line & support trenches.	RBB
"	8th	—	As above. The Party of Sixty men under 2/Lt R.W.Bradley continued the work at the G.H.Q. 2nd Line.	RBB
"	9th	—	D Coy. moved from YPRES to Redoubt T.28 d.3.9 and worked on reclaiming an obsolete communication trench.	RBB
"	10th	—	D Coy. continued the work commenced yesterday. A Party of 90 men under 2/Lt R.W.Bradley continued the wiring of the G.H.Q. 2nd Line.	RBB
"	11th	—	The Battalion was disposed as above.	RBB

Army Form C. 2118.

WAR DIARY
or
INTELLIGENCE SUMMARY.

(Erase heading not required.)

March 1916.

45/

Place	Date	Hour	Summary of Events and Information	Remarks and references to Appendices
DICKEBUSCH	12th.	—	Wkg. Party of 120 men continued the work of reclaiming the communication trench.	App.
		—	The party of 30 men left Brasky continued the work of wiring to the C.H.Q. subline.	App.
	13th.	—	B Company relieved A Company at BEDFORD HOUSE	
	14th.	—	A Company paraded as strong as possible and proceeded by Buses to KRUISSTRAAT H18 C.9.1. there they were met by Capt. McQueen, 7th Field Coy. R.E. who guided them to I28B.7.4. They worked from 8p.m. - 1p.m. in reclaiming and revetting Johnson Street, an old communication trench.	App.
	15th.	—	A Company paraded at 5.30p.m. and proceeded to I28B.7.4. where they continued the work of reclaiming Johnson Street.	App.
	16th.	—	A Company paraded as above and proceeded to I28B.7.4. where they continued the work of reclaiming revetting Johnson Street.	App.

WAR DIARY
or
INTELLIGENCE SUMMARY.

(Erase heading not required.)

Army Form C. 2118.

March 1916.

Place	Date	Hour	Summary of Events and Information	Remarks and references to Appendices
DICKEBUSCH	17th	—	The three forward Companies (A, C, D) are working at very high pressure. Their work – which is mainly night work – consists almost entirely in revetting communication trenches, and in making wire intanglements in front of the support and reserve trenches.	R.A.B
"	"	"	As above.	R.A.B
"	18th	"	As above.	R.A.B
"	19th	"	The Band played a Programme at Canada Huts.	R.A.B
"	20th	—	A Company relieved D Company in YPRES. A Coy. was conveyed in buses as far as the R.E. Dump at KRUISSTRAAT. From there left-handed took the bay to R.7. I.28.a.3.9. where he arrived at 9 p.m. The Company worked till 1.30 a.m. on revetting and draining on the communication trench Johnson Street, and returned to their Billets in the YPRES Magazine, arriving there at 3.30 a.m.	R.A.B
"	21st	"	As above.	
"	22nd	"	As above.	A.B

Army Form C. 2118.

WAR DIARY
or
INTELLIGENCE SUMMARY.

(Erase heading not required.)

#7. March 1916.

Place	Date	Hour	Summary of Events and Information	Remarks and references to Appendices
DICKEBUSCH	23rd		D Company moved to CANAL DUGOUTS.	App33.
"	"		A Company moved to SWAN CHATEAU.	
"	"		Both of these Companies became attached to the 15th Infantry Brigade. Sir Douglas Haig visited Canadian Huts.	App33
"	24th		A + D Companies continued their new work near de BLUFF. The work consisted in strengthening and rectifying the communication trenches from the support to the front line, and in rebuilding and drawing the support line.	App.
"	"		Two platoons of B Coy. under Lt. H.Stewart returned to CANADA HUTS.	App.
"	25th		As above.	
"	26th		Orders were received that Headquarters & two Companies of the Battalion were to relieve the 5th Border Regt. in the trenches on the night of the 27/28th March.	App.
"	27th		The Battalion (less B + C Companies) relieved the 5th Border Regt. in trenches 32, 33 + 34 (Just north of the YPRES - COMINES Canal)	App.

1577 Wt.W10791/1773 500,000 1/15 D. D. & L. A.D.S.S./Forms/C. 2118.

Army Form C. 2118.

WAR DIARY
or
INTELLIGENCE SUMMARY.
(Erase heading not required.)

48.   March 1916.

Place	Date	Hour	Summary of Events and Information	Remarks and references to Appendices
DICKEBUSCH	28th	—	In trenches as above. A very quiet day. The Companies carried out excellent work and improved the state of the trenches considerably	MSB
"	29th	—	C Company returned to CANADA HUTS. The Battalion (less C & B Coys) was in trenches as above.	MSB
"	30th	—	B Coy (less two platoons) returned to CANADA HUTS. The Battalion (less C & B Coys) remained in trenches as above.	RBS
"	31st	—	The Battalion (less B & C Coys) was relieved by St Bede Regt. & returned to CANADA HUTS. Excellent work had been done by Bn. Gen. Sec. Cos. D.S.O. while in the trenches, and the highest terms praised the Battalion in the lightest terms	

RBS ratten
Capt/Adjt.
1st (Pioneers)

WAR DIARY
or
INTELLIGENCE SUMMARY.

Army Form C. 2118.

#9 April/1916.

Place	Date	Hour	Summary of Events and Information	Remarks and references to Appendices
DICKEBUSCH HUTS.	1st	—	C Company (attached to 149th Infantry Brigade) moved to R.E. Farm (Mrs REMY'S).	
"	2nd	—	As above.	
"	3rd	—	As above.	
"	4th	—	The Battalion (less C & 2 Platoons B Coy) marched via Reninghelst to SCHERPENBERG. The Battalion marched in threes and this formation was found to be suitable to the narrow roads.	
SCHERPENBERG	5th	—	A Company proceeded to N.12 — a reserve trench — behind the 151st Infantry Brigade Sector and worked for 5 hours on building a new parapet.	
"	6th	"	A Company moved to RIDGWOOD DUGOUTS.	
"	7th	"	The work A Company is doing consists in revetting and strengthening the reserve trench N.12.	
"	"	"	B Company is revetting and drawing REGENT ST. and VIA GELLIA communication trenches.	
"	"	"	C Company is revetting and making bridge traverses in HATZING ST. communication trench.	

Army Form C. 2118.

WAR DIARY
or
INTELLIGENCE SUMMARY.
(Erase heading not required.)

50/ April 1916

Place	Date	Hour	Summary of Events and Information	Remarks and references to Appendices
SCHERPENBERG	8th	—	As above.	RBB
"	9th	—	Church Parade for HQrs. & D Company.	
"	10th	—	D Company relieved C Company in huts near R.E. FARM. Lieut. Laing with a party of fifty commenced work on the SCHERPENBERG Defences. This work consisted in building overhead cover to the M. Gun Emplacements, and in revetting the two sides of the trenches.	RBB
"	10th	"	As above.	
"	11th	"	C Company moved to R.E. Farm to carry out special work on the front line of the 149th. Infantry Brigade. This work consists in joining up several isolated posts.	RBB
"	12th	"	Work continued as above.	
"	13th	"	Work continued as above.	
"	14th	"	A boy mines the front line trench which led the enemy heavily bombarded throughout the day.	RBB
"	15th	"	M Coy. continued the work of repairing the front line which they had been again badly treated. The work which they	RBB

Army Form C. 2118.

WAR DIARY
or
INTELLIGENCE SUMMARY.
(Erase heading not required.)

5/ April 1916.

Instructions regarding War Diaries and Intelligence Summaries are contained in F.S. Regs., Part II. and the Staff Manual respectively. Title pages will be prepared in manuscript.

Place	Date	Hour	Summary of Events and Information	Remarks and references to Appendices
SCHERPENBERG	16th	—	was excellent although not carried out under intermittent machine gun fire.	App
	19th	—	The Companies continues the work matured above.	App
	18th	—	As above.	
	19th	—	The Sears Gun Detachment are working daily in the SCHERPEN-BERG Defences. The work consists in revetting the sides of the trenches, improving the drainage system, and constructing overhead cover for the Machine Gun Emplacements.	App
	20th	—	As above.	
	21st	—	A Company's work was interrupted by continuously machine gun and artillery fire. Nevertheless quite an appreciable amount was carried out. The work consisted in rebuilding an obsolete Support line.	App
	22nd	—	A Company returned to Hays.	App
	23rd	—	B Coy. is still engaged in making a new communication trench from the Indian Reg. - Kemmel road to Regent St. Dugout. This trench is on the left of Regent Street, and as it	App

WAR DIARY or INTELLIGENCE SUMMARY.

Army Form C. 2118.

52.

April 1916.

Place	Date	Hour	Summary of Events and Information	Remarks and references to Appendices
SCHERPENBERG	23rd	—	is in full view of WYTSCHAETE & work is somewhat hampered by still fire.	AAR
"	"	"	B and C companies – attached to the 147th Inf. Brigade – are engaged on similar work. This work consists in linking up posts of the front line which we is taken and in rebuilding two isolated support trenches. The men are working in very wet places and find difficult conditions at night, yet the work they are doing is of a very high standard and bear the full mark of the "finish" its above.	AAR
"	"	"		AAR
"	24th	"	B and C Companies returned to Hays.	AAR
"	25th	—	The Battalion moved to a tent camp in LA CLYTTE with the exception of B Coy. A Coy & D Coy proceeded to work on the VIERSTRAAT SWITCH. This work consists of revering an old trench–clearing it and revetting. A Coy worked on the left of VIERSTRAAT and D Coy on the right of A.	
LA CLYTTE	26th	—		N.F.L.

Army Form C. 2118.

WAR DIARY
or
INTELLIGENCE SUMMARY.
(Erase heading not required.)

53.

April 1916

Place	Date	Hour	Summary of Events and Information	Remarks and references to Appendices
LACYTE	27th		A Coy worked on the right Sector of VIERSTRAAT SWITCH	W.P.Q.
	28th		A Coy worked on the left Sector and D Coy on the right. B Coy returned to the Camp. The Commanding Officer held a Field Kit inspection of D Coy.	W.P.Q.
	29th		B Coy worked on the left Sector and C Coy on the right. The Commanding Officer inspected C Coy. The Band reported to 50th Division at FLETRE.	W.P.Q.
	30th		A Coy worked on the left Sector and C Coy on the right. Church Parade was held in the Camp - all Companies being present. An Official photographer took several photographs of the men in skeleton order wearing their Steel Helmets.	W.P.Q.

1/7 Durham L.I. 5B
54
May 1916 Vol 13

WAR DIARY
or
INTELLIGENCE SUMMARY.

Army Form C. 2118.

Pioneers

Place	Date	Hour	Summary of Events and Information	Remarks and references to Appendices
LA CLYTE	1st		B Coy & C Coy worked as above.	N.T.R.
"	2nd		A Coy & D Coy as above. The work is considerably hindered by the water in trench which makes the placing of "U" frames difficult.	N.T.R.
"	3rd		Officers Commanding Coys of the 9th D.L.I. arrived this afternoon and ascertained full particulars of the work with a view to taking over tomorrow. B Coy and C Coy worked as above.	
METEREN AREA	4th		The Battalion marched to rest area about 1 mile due East of FLETRE, a distance of ten miles. The Divisional Band met the Battalion at METEREN. The Billets are very good Farm Buildings but somewhat scattered. Headquarters (27.X.1.D.3.3.) and D Coy being on the NORTH side of the road METEREN–FLETRE and the remaining Coys on the South Side.	N.T.R.
"	5th		At rest Billets as above –	N.T.R.
"	6th		As above. A cricket match was played this afternoon between the Officers and N.C.O's and men, resulting in a win for the N.C.O's and men.	N.T.R.

Army Form C. 2118.

WAR DIARY
or
INTELLIGENCE SUMMARY.
(Erase heading not required.)

5 5 / May 1916

Place	Date	Hour	Summary of Events and Information	Remarks and references to Appendices
METEREN	7th		As above. Church Parade was cancelled on account of the wet.	W.P.K.
"	8th		Battalion Training commenced this morning. The time was devoted to "Handling of Arms" and Squad Drill. 16 men under 2nd Lt. H. Thompson started a course of training for Scouts. Spare men were attached to the Lewis Gun Detachment, Signal Section and Medical Officer for special instruction.	
"	9th		Training as above.	W.P.K. / A.P.K.
"	10th		As above. The Battalion paraded at 11 o/c for Battalion Drill under the Commanding Officer.	A.P.K. / A.P.K.
"	11th		Training as above.	
"	12th		All men who had not been inoculated during the last twelve months were inoculated this morning.	A.P.K. / A.P.K.
"	13th		The Battalion rested after inoculation.	
"	14th		Holy Communion was held at D Company's Billet this morning. Parade Service was cancelled on account of the wet.	N.P.K.
"	15th		Training as above.	N.P.K.

Army Form C. 2118.

WAR DIARY
or
INTELLIGENCE SUMMARY.
(Erase heading not required.)

56/

May 1916.

Place	Date	Hour	Summary of Events and Information	Remarks and references to Appendices
METEREN	16th		Major General Shea C.B., D.S.O. held a Farewell Parade of the 151st Infantry Brigade before his departure to take up command of a Division. The Battalion was present. In the course of his address Major General Shea thanked the parade for all the splendid work they had done while under his command. In the afternoon Battalion Sports were held. The Battalion carried out a Route March of six miles. Sports for Divisional Troops (organised by the Battalion) were held in field.	W.D.K. [?]
"	17th 18th		Training as above.	W.D.K. [?]
"	19th			
M.A.CLYTTE	20th		The Battalion relieved the 5th YORKS at the Camp LA CLYTTE. B & D Coys commenced work on VIERSTRAAT SWITCH. The work consists of retrieving an old trench - revetting with U Frames & strengthening parados and parapets.	W.D.K.
"	21st		A & C Coys worked as above. Parade Service was held in Camp.	W.D.K.
"	22nd		B & D Coys worked as above.	W.D.K.

Army Form C. 2118.

WAR DIARY
or
INTELLIGENCE SUMMARY.
(Erase heading not required.)

5? / May 1916.

Place	Date	Hour	Summary of Events and Information	Remarks and references to Appendices
LACLYTTE	23rd		The Battalion relieved the 20th K.R.R. at Huts SCHERPENBERG. A & C Coy worked under the 3rd Division on the Front Line. The work consisted chiefly of connecting up the R & L Trenches by means of Sandbag work.	W.J.L.
SCHERPENBERG	24th		B & D Coy worked as above. C Coy proceeded to R.E Farm for work under the 149th Infantry Brigade in conjunction with the 1st Field Company R.E. to work chiefly on raising the parapets of the Rhondda N.J.L	N.J.L
"	25"		A Coy did a nights work on repairing NATLING STREET. The Enemys Bombardment had caused several gaps in the J trenches and half of B Coy and half of D Coy did the necessary repair work.	J.J.L
"	26.		The remaining half Companies of B & D Continued work on the J trenches	G.J.L
"	27"		A Coy moved to RIDGE WOOD Dug-outs for work under the 151st Inf. Brigade in conjunction with the 7th Field Coy. R.E. D Coy moved to Forward Billets under direction from 150th Inf Brigade to work in conjunction with the 2nd Field Coy. R.E. Half Coy. Billeted in KEMMEL and half in REGENT STREET DUGOUTS. The Divisional Band	

Army Form C. 2118.

WAR DIARY
or
INTELLIGENCE SUMMARY.

(Erase heading not required.)

Place	Date	Hour	Summary of Events and Information	Remarks and references to Appendices
SCHERPENBERG	27th		reported for duty.	W.P.L.
"	28th		Church Parade was held at the Huts. In the afternoon B Coy proceeded to R.E. FARM for work in Centre Sects under the 149. Inf. Brigade	J.P.L.
"	29th		The Band proceeded to 2nd Army School at WISQUES for a fortnight	W.P.L.
"	30th		As above. A day's work consists of retrieving communication trench POPPY LANE. C Coy & B Coy are connecting up etc. J. the "K" trenches. This work is rendered somewhat difficult the trench mortars of the enemy. D Coy is employed in delivering support line from PIROG 1 L 10 to REGENT STREET.	J.P.L.
"	31st		As above. The Lewis Gun Section has furnished guards over the Coast and assisted the Carpenters in erecting latrines in the Camp.	W.P.L.

1577 Wt. W10791/1773 500,000 1/15 D.D. & L. A.D.S.S./Forms/C. 2118.

WAR DIARY or INTELLIGENCE SUMMARY

Army Form C. 2118.

June 1916

Place	Date	Hour	Summary of Events and Information	Remarks and references to Appendices
SCHERPENBERG	1st		A Company continues work on POPPY LANE - heightening sides and revetting with 'U' frames. B Company continues work of strengthening parapets and parados of the K1 and M trenches. C Company continues reclaiming trenches K1-K2a. D Company continues work of Subsidiary Line between VIA GELLIA and REGENTSTREET.	W.F.K.
	2nd		As above	W.F.K.
	3rd		As above	W.F.K.
	4th		Church of England Parade was held at SCHERPENBERG HUTS for Headquarters and Details.	W.F.K.
	5th		The following awards have appeared in the Battalion Honours. The Commanding Officer C.M.G., N° 2276 Sergeant Bothwick D.M., D.C.M., N° 1720 Pte Nash A. Military medal. — Lieut Colonel Stuart of the Divisional Staff, who was killed last night, was buried this afternoon in WESTOUTRE. The Battalion provided the carrying party, firing party and Buglers.	
	6th		The Companies worked as above -	W.F.K.

Army Form C. 2118.

WAR DIARY
or
INTELLIGENCE SUMMARY.
(Erase heading not required.)

60
June 1916

Place	Date	Hour	Summary of Events and Information	Remarks and references to Appendices
SCHERPENBERG	7th		As above. C Coy commenced work on new support line behind K 2 b and K 2 a - digging out and fitting U Frames	W.F.L.
	8th		As above.	W.F.L.
	9th		As above.	W.F.L.
	10th		As above.	W.F.L.
	11th		Church of England Parade was held at Headquarters. Work as above. The Lewis Gun Section proceeded to R.E. Farm under Captain R.G. Macintyre for work with the 149th Infantry Brigade. The Divisional Band returned from WISQUES.	W.F.L.
	12th			W.F.L.
	13th		The Lewis Gun Section commenced work on ROSSIGNOL AVENUE	W.F.L.
	14th		The Bandsmen commenced work at KEMMEL erecting new huts.	W.F.L.
	15th		The Commanding Officer was mentioned in General Sir Douglas Haigs Despatch.	W.F.L.
	16th		Work as above.	W.F.L.
	17th		As above.	W.F.L.
	18th		Church of England Parade was held at Headquarters.	W.F.L.

Army Form C. 2118.

WAR DIARY
INTELLIGENCE SUMMARY.
(Erase heading not required.)

61.
June 1916.

Place	Date	Hour	Summary of Events and Information	Remarks and references to Appendices
SCHERPENBERG	19th		As above.	W.P.L.
	20th		D Company moved from night Sector to Billets near LA CLYTTE and were attached to the 151st Infantry Brigade.	W.P.L.
	21st		As above.	
	22nd		D Company commenced work on POPPYLANE. The work consists of making out digging and erecting wire U frames parts of the communication trench.	W.P.L.
	23rd		The work on both sectors is rendered very difficult by the heavy rains making the approach to the work heavy.	W.P.L.
	24th		As above	W.P.L.
	25th		Church of England Parade Service was held at Headquarters	W.P.L.
	26th		As above.	W.P.L.
	27th		As above	W.P.L.
	29th		As above.	W.P.L.
	30th		Very little work has been done this week on account of the heavy bombardment along the Division front.	W.P.L.

W. P. Laing
Lieut & Adjutant

ORIGINAL.

WAR DIARY.

7th Battalion (Pioneers)
DURHAM LIGHT INFANTRY.

JULY. 1916.

VOLUME No.

WAR DIARY or INTELLIGENCE SUMMARY

Army Form C. 2118.

7th Bn Durham Light Infantry (Pioneers)

July 1916. (p. 62)

Place	Date	Hour	Summary of Events and Information	Remarks and references to Appendices
SCHERPENBERG	1st		B and C Companies continue work on new Support Line behind the K.1.b trenches - A and D Coys are working on POPPY LANE Communication trench.	W.?.2.
	2nd		In addition the Lewis Gun Detach went to working on the New Support Line	W.?.2.
	3rd		Church of England Parade Service was held at Head quarters. D Company moved from FAIRY DELL 28. N.13. a 5.5 to tent camp in LA CLYTTE.	W.?.2.
	4th		D Company moved from tent camp to a field on the West side of SCHERPENBERG - LA CLYTTE ROAD. 28. N.7.C. 5.9.	W.?.2.
	5th		work as above.	W.?.2.
	6th		A and D Companies continue work on POPPY LANE - deepening and clearing trench, fitting U frames, revetting trench and fitting grids. B and C Companies continue work on New Support Line and B Company	W.?.2.
	7		on Communication trench to K.2.b	W.?.2.
	8		As above.	W.?.2.
	9		Church of England Parade Service was held at Headquarters	W.?.2.
	10		B Company commenced deepening Support Line from H9 to ROSSIGNOL AVENUE.	W.?.2.

WAR DIARY
INTELLIGENCE SUMMARY.

Army Form C. 2118.

July 1916

63

Place	Date	Hour	Summary of Events and Information	Remarks and references to Appendices
SCHERPENBERG	10th		A Company moved from RIDGEWOOD to D Company's Billet in LACLYTTE and D Company took over A Company's Billet	W.D.L.
	11th		As above - D Company revetted new arm of POPPYLANE to WYTSCHAETE BECK and left flank walk along the BECK to VIERSTRAAT ROAD.	W.D.L.
	12th		As above	W.D.L.
	13th		B Company continued work on Support Line from H.4 to ROSSIGNOL AVENUE	W.D.L.
	14th		As above	W.D.L.
	15th		As above	W.D.L.
	16th		Church of England Service held at Headquarters	W.D.L.
	17th		As above	W.D.L.
	18th		As above.	W.D.L.
	19th		The Lewis Gun Detachments arrived at Headquarters and the training of men for Six Detachments commenced under the Lewis Gun Officer.	W.D.L.
	20th		As above -	W.D.L.
	21st		As above.	W.D.L.
	22nd		A Company moved from LACLYTTE to Billets near DRANOUTRE	W.D.L.

Army Form C. 2118.

WAR DIARY
or
INTELLIGENCE SUMMARY.
(Erase heading not required.)

July 1916   64

Place	Date	Hour	Summary of Events and Information	Remarks and references to Appendices
SCHERPENBERG	22nd		(28) M 36 b.0.5. for work with 149th Infantry Brigade and D Company moved from RIDGEWOOD to LOCREHOF FARM for work with the 151st Infantry Brigade	W.F.L.
	23rd		Church of England Parade Service held at Headquarters.	W.F.L.
	24th		D Company commenced work in New Support Line from VIA GELLIA to PALL MALL. U Training Revetting and Flooring – Completing new Dug outs in KITCHEN AVENUE and YOUNG STREET. A Company worked in the BUTTS behind D3 D2 and D1 Cleaning shell trench –	
	25th		D Company moved to billets at 28. N. 25. c. 2. 8	W.F.L.
	26th		Companies worked as above –	W.F.L.
	27th		Half of A Company moved to forward Billets at 28 T 3 b. 9. 3.	W.F.L.
	28th		Companies worked as above – A Company retained SPRING WALK.	W.F.L.
	29th		As above –	W.F.L.
	30th		Church of England Parade Service held at Headquarters – Remainder of A Company moved to Forward Billets – 28. N. 25. c. 2. 8 –	W.F.L.
	31st		As above –	W.F.L.

J. F. Lewis
Lieut ? D.L.I. (Durrenin)

Operation Orders

B.M. = BAILLEUL MAIN
G = GODEWAERSVELDE
D.N. = DOULLENS NORTH
F.C. = FIENVILLERS CANDAS

1. The Battalion will entrain on Friday morning 11/8/16.
2. 'A' Coy and 4 G.S. Wagons (Tools) will leave B.M. at 8.58 a.m. in N° 13 Train and detraining at D.N.
3. The 4 G.S. Wagons will arrive at B.M. at 6 a.m. and 'A' Coy will arrive at 7.30 A.M.
   O.C. 'A' Coy will hand in to R.T.O. on arrival a complete marching out State showing Numbers of men, horses, and 4 Wheeled Wagons, a duplicate will be handed into Orderly Room as the Company passes.
   The Transport Officer will render a parade State to O.C. 'A' Coy by 9 p.m. on Thursday night showing the number of men, horses and 4 Wheeled Wagons which will accompany 'A' Coy.
4. An Officer from 'A' Coy will report at B.M at 5.50 a.m. to an Officer from Divisional Headqrs to receive instructions as regards the procedure to be adopted when the wagons and Company arrive.
5. <u>The remainder of the Battalion</u> will leave G at 10.53 a.m. in train N° 15 and detraining at F.C.
6. 'B' Coy and remainder of Transport will arrive at G at 8 a.m. and the remainder of the Battalion will parade at Battalion Alarm Post at 7.15 a.m.
   O.C. 'B' Coy will hand to R.T.O. on arrival a complete marching out State which will be given him by the Adjutant when the

company moves off.

6. 'B', 'C', 'D' Coys and Details will render to Orderly Room by 6 a.m. a marching out state showing number of men, horses, 4 wheeled wagons and 2 wheeled wagons and bicycles.

7. An Officer from 'B' Coy will report at G at 7.50 a.m. to an Officer from Divisional Headqrs to receive instructions as regards the procedure to be adopted when the remainder of the Battalion arrives.

8. The entrainment must be completed half an hour before the time of departure of train.

9. No troops or transport will enter the Station Yard until authorised to do so by the R.T.O.

10. No personnel or stores will be allowed in the brake vans at each end of the trains.

11. Supply and Baggage wagons will accompany the Transport.

12. RATIONS – The Battalion will entrain with the unexpended portion of Friday's rations and the Train Vehicles loaded with rations for consumption on the 12th inst.

13. Water Bottles must be carried and water carts entrained full.

14. Breast ropes for horse trucks must be provided by the Transport Officer. Ropes for lashing vehicles will be provided by the Railway.

15. Each Coy. will detail three men to ensure that once the entrainment is completed no one leaves the train without permission until ordered to do so at the Station of detrainment.

16. The approximate time of journey is 6 hours.

Original.

SECRET.

WAR DIARY.
of
7th Battn. Durham Light Infantry (Pioneers)

Volume XVII.

From 1st to 31st August, 1916.

WAR DIARY

7th Bn DURHAM LIGHT INFANTRY PIONEERS

INTELLIGENCE SUMMARY
AUGUST 1916

VOLUME NUMBER 17

Army Form C. 2118.

Place	Date	Hour	Summary of Events and Information	Remarks and references to Appendices
SCHERPENBERG	1st		A Company continues work on "the Butts" behind the F trenches B Company on Support line from H4 to ROSSIGNOL AVENUE C Company in trenches J10 and J2 and D Company on New Support line between VIA GELLIA and PALL MALL	
"	2nd		As above	9.7.2.
"	3rd		As above	9.7.2.
"	4th		As above	9.7.2.
"	5th		As above	9.7.2.
"	6th		Church of England Parade Service held at Headquarters. All Companies arrived at Headquarters, being relieved by the 5th Bn SOUTH WALES BORDERERS (PIONEERS.)	9.7.2.
FLETRE	7th		The Battalion moved to Reserve area at FLETRE. Headquarters at SHEET 27 N 18 B. 2.6. and the remainder of the Battalion in neighbouring farms.	9.7.2. 9.7.2. 9.7.2.
"	8th		Today was spent in examining the equipment of the men.	
"	9th		Companies carried out a five mile Route March this morning.	

Army Form C. 2118.

WAR DIARY
or
INTELLIGENCE SUMMARY.
(Erase heading not required.)

Instructions regarding War Diaries and Intelligence Summaries are contained in F. S. Regs., Part II. and the Staff Manual respectively. Title pages will be prepared in manuscript.

Place	Date	Hour	Summary of Events and Information	Remarks and references to Appendices
FLETRE	10th		Battalion prepared for entraining.	W.D.R.
"	11th		Battalion entrained – vide Operation orders attached and marched to Billets in BERNEUIL reference LENS 11.	W.D.R.
BERNEUIL	12th		In Billets	W.D.R.
"	13th		Church of England Parade Service was held.	W.D.R.
"	14th		Battalion carried out a ROUTE MARCH of five miles	W.D.R.
"	15th		Battalion marched to Billets in VIGNACOURT. [Lens 11.]	W.D.R.
VIGNACOURT	16th		Battalion marched to Billets in PIERREGOT. [Lens 11.] – Billets were very scarce and the majority of men slept in shelters.	W.D.R.
PIERREGOT	17th		Battalion marched to Billets in BAIZIEUX 62D – C.6.c.2.3.	W.D.R.
BAIZIEUX	18th		In Billets as above –	W.D.R.
"	19th		Battalion training commenced – particular attention being given to the fitness of the men and his cupline	W.D.R.
"	20th		Church of England Parade Service was held.	W.D.R.
"	21st		Training as above	W.D.R.
"	22nd		As above	W.D.R.

WAR DIARY
or
INTELLIGENCE SUMMARY.
(Erase heading not required.)

Army Form C. 2118.

Place	Date	Hour	Summary of Events and Information	Remarks and references to Appendices
BAIZIEUX	23rd		Training as above	W.I.K.
"	24th		All Companies commenced work on Cruciform String Posts.	W.I.K.
"	25th		As above.	
"	26th		A Company and C Company proceeded under Major W.D.C. HUNT to BECOURT 57D S.E. X 25 C 5.5 – at were attached to C.R.E 15th Division.	
"	27th		These two Companies commenced work repairing tram line from BOTTOM WOOD to CONTALMAISON and repairing roads in MAMETZ WOOD area. 100 hrs from the remaining Companies worked on new road running through HENENCOURT WOOD 57D V 26 b.3.4.	W.I.K.
"	28th		Church of England Parade Service was held at headquarters. As above – h 65 - C.S.M. STOKER J. was presented with the D.C.M by Lieutenant General Sir. W.P. PULTENEY, K.C.B., D.S.O.	W.I.K. W.I.K. W.I.K.
"	29th		Work was continued as above.	
"	30th		As above	
"	31st		As above.	

J. J. Lane
Capt & Adjutant
D.L.I. (Pioneers)

7th. DURHAM LIGHT INFANTRY

(PIONEERS)

50th. DIVISION

SEPTEMBER 1916.

17. Officers chargers will accompany the Transport.

18. Officers valises, mess kit, blankets, Dixies &c must be ready at entrance to Billets at 3-30 a.m. for collection.

Sgnd. W. F. Laing.
Capt. & Adjutant.
7th D.L.I. (Pioneers).

ORIGINAL.   SECRET.

WAR DIARY.

of

7th Battalion (Pioneers)

Durham Light Infantry.

September, 1916.

Volume No. XVlll.

-a-a-a-a-a-a-a-a-a-a-a-a-a-

WAR DIARY or INTELLIGENCE SUMMARY.

Army Form C. 2118.

7th Bn DURHAM LIGHT INFANTRY (PIONEERS)

SEPTEMBER 1916   N° 18

Place	Date	Hour	Summary of Events and Information	Remarks and references to Appendices
BAIZIEUX	1st		Remainder of Battalion continued training. A Coy continued road repairing MARTIN PUICH - CONTALMAISON ROADS. C Coy on tramway at SHELTER WOOD. 100 men continued work on road through HENENCOURT WOOD. Sheets 57D & 62D.	W.7.4.
	2nd		As above - A Party of 40 men commenced work on Divisional Headquarters at D.6.6.1.3. 62 D.	W.7.4. W.7.2.
	3rd		As above. Church of England parade was held at Headquarters	
BECOURT.	4th		The remainder of the Battalion moved forward under orders of 15th Division. Headquarters at BECOURT 62 D. F.1.b.9.0. Quartermasters Stores and Transport ALBERT 62 D. F.3.d.5.2. B Coy D Coy and Lewis Gun Detachment in Bivy Outs at 57D. X.23d central.	W.7.4. W.7.9.
	5th		As above -	
	6th		D Coy Commenced work on BETHEL SAP and ARGYLL & SUTHERLAND TRENC and B Coy on JUTLAND EXTENSION and KERRY ALLEY - cleaning deepening and trench bonding - the work is continually hindered by shell fire.	W.7.9.

Army Form C. 2118.

WAR DIARY
or
INTELLIGENCE SUMMARY.
(Erase heading not required.)

Place	Date	Hour	Summary of Events and Information	Remarks and references to Appendices
BECOURT	7th		As above. The Lewis Gun Detachment were attached to D Coy for work	W.7.E.
	8th		As above. C & D Coys continued work on CONTALMAISON-LONGUEVAL ROAD. The road is in very bad condition and requires a great deal of metal.	W.7.E.
	9th		Platoon of A Coy commenced work on "A" Bomb Dump. X.25.c.3.5. 27D. Other parties worked as above.	W.7.E.
	10th		B Coy company were very much hindered by shelling while working on JUTLAND SAP.	W.7.E.
	11th		A Coy & C Coy. continued work on roads. D Coy took over work on SOMME ALLEY.	W.7.E.
	12th		as above.	W.7.E.
	13th		as above.	W.7.E.
FRICOURT	14th		The Battalion moved forward to take part in the offensive and were distributed as follows – Headquarters Lewis Gun Detachment A Coy and half of C Coy at reserve trenches at 57D. X.27.B & X.28.a. D Coy to LANCS TRENCH	

WAR DIARY or INTELLIGENCE SUMMARY

Army Form C. 2118.

Place	Date	Hour	Summary of Events and Information	Remarks and references to Appendices
FRICOURT	14th		S.2.D.57c. B Coy to S.P.B.2.3 (57c) and remainder of C Coy to 6 x 29 B.S.S. B Coy were attached to 149th Infantry Brigade and D Coy attached 150th Infantry Brigade O.O. attached.	W.2.R.
	15th		In the afternoon of the attack D Coy dug a C.T. under very heavy shell fire from PIONEER ALLEY to TANGLE TRENCH S.2.B. 2 Platoons of C Coy with the 7th Field Coy repaired the road from BAZENTIN-LE-PETIT towards HIGH WOOD. B Coy were employed in digging gun emplacements and trench for Howitzer Battery at S.8.B.3.3.	W.2.R.
	16th		A Coy relieved C Coy on the road where relief progress has been made – D Coy proceed to BAZENTIN-LE-PETIT WOOD S.7.D.3.3 57c and dug a C.T. to the N.E. CORNER of MARTIN PUICH from MARTIN ALLEY. B Coy Completes BETHEL S.A.P. to German Old Line and cleared CRESCENT ALLEY for a distance of 800 yards to a point by Sunken Road. C Coy relieved A Coy on the road – Each worked for 12 hours.	W.2.R.
	17th		A Combined party of 95 men from A & C Coys with the 2nd Field Coy dug a CRUCIFORM Strong Post about S.3.B.9.7 in conjunction with B Coy dug 400 yards of C.T. from ground level connecting EYE TRENCH with HOOK TRENCH and 60 yards forward from HOOK TRENCH. A Small party from D Coy under LIEUT. N.R. SHEPHERD dug a Strong Post in the CRESCENT which had been	

1577 Wt.W10791/1773 500,000 1/15 D. D. & L. A.D.S.S./Forms/C. 2118.

Army Form C. 2118.

WAR DIARY
or
INTELLIGENCE SUMMARY.
(Erase heading not required.)

Place	Date	Hour	Summary of Events and Information	Remarks and references to Appendices
FRICOURT	17th		Taken over the Division this afternoon about M.33.B.7.5.	B.7.L
	18th		Work continued on the Road by A&C Coys. A party from Steen two Coys 10 Stray with the 1st Field Coy dug a new trench 4.5'x2.5' between M.34.C.2.8 & M.34.a.7.3. B Coy dug 200 yards of this trench - the C.R.E. congratulated the Battalion on this splendid work. D Coy connected up MARTIN TRENCH with CRESCENT ALLEY.	B.7.K
	19th		A & C Coys continued work on road which is passable for transport 200 yards N.W. of HIGH WOOD. B Coy Dug 150 yards of JUTLAND ALLEY extension to HOOK TRENCH and finished RUTHERFORD ALLEY. The Divisional Band has provided daily parties for loading wagons for the team work.	M.7.K
	20th		C Coy relieved B Coy today and A Coy continued work on the Road - owing to heavy transport the road from CONTALMAISON CUTTING to HIGH WOOD requires a great deal of repairing daily.	M.7.Q
	21st		A Coy relieved D Coy who returned to Billets at X.29.B.5.8. A Coy dug C.T. between STARFISH & PRUE TRENCH. and D Coy continued work on RUTHERFORD ALLEY - Widening, deepening and Trench Boarding.	M.7.Q

WAR DIARY
or
INTELLIGENCE SUMMARY.
(Erase heading not required.)

Army Form C. 2118.

Place	Date	Hour	Summary of Events and Information	Remarks and references to Appendices
FRICOURT.	22"		C Coy dug 200 yards of new trench from NUTLAND ALLEY towards HOOK TRENCH. D Coy continued work on RUTHERFORD ALLEY and B Coy on the road from BAZENTIN-LE-PETIT to HIGH WOOD.	W.F.R.
	23"		Work continued as above. RUTHERFORD ALLEY is now Trench Boarded to the BOW. Trench Boards have been laid in CRESCENT ALLEY to SUNKEN ROAD.	W.F.R. W.F.R.
	24"		As above -	
	25"		RUTHERFORD ALLEY has been Trench Boarded up to STARFISH LINE & D Co - CRESCENT ALLEY has been Cleared to PRUE TRENCH & C Coy. RUTHERFORD ALLEY has been extended 350 yards. in part of PRUE Trench by A Coy. B Coy Continued work from THE CUTTING to HIGH WOOD	W.F.R.
	26"		Work as above. C Coy Changed Billets to S.7.D.2.2.	W.F.R.
	27"		As above -	
	28"		RUTHERFORD ALLEY is now Completed to PRUE TRENCH and from this point to M.28.D.7.8. dug to a depth of four feet - CRESCENT	

Army Form C. 2118.

WAR DIARY
or
INTELLIGENCE SUMMARY.
(Erase heading not required.)

Place	Date	Hour	Summary of Events and Information	Remarks and references to Appendices
FRICOURT	28th		ALLEY is not cleared to M.27.D.6.9.	R.7.F.
	29th		Work continued as above. B Coy have been working daily on communications BAZENTIN-le-PETIT to MARTINPUICH and to HIGH WOOD	R.7.F.
	30th		A Coy with 200 Infantry continued RUTHERFORD ALLEY to new JUMPING OFF Trench about M.22.D.O.8. The remaining Coys worked as above.	R.2.F.

N.F. Laing
Captain, Adjutant
7.B. (Pioneers)
7/B: Durham Light Infantry

(Secret)

Operation Order No. 2.

Reference Map 1/40,000
Sheets 57c, 57d. 62d.
and French Map.

1. (a) The Fourth Army in conjunction with the French and the Reserve Army is going to renew the attack on Friday 15th Sept.

   (b) The 50th Division will attack with the 47th Division on its right and the 15th Division on its left.

2. (a) The final objective of the 50th Division is a line from M.34.b.5.9 — M.33.a.4.6 — M.33.c.1.9 — M.32.d.7.8 — S.2.b.2.9.

   (b) This objective will be reached in three bounds. The first bound is to the line (BROWN) S.3.b.8.9 — M.32.d.9.4. — M.32.d.2.7.

   The second bound is to the line (GREEN) M.34.b.2.1. — M.33.b.7.2. — M.33.c.8.9. — M.32.d.7.7 — M.32.d.2.7.

   The third bound is to the line (BLUE) COPSE (M.34.b.3.8) (inclusive) — M.33.a.9.8. — M.33.a.4.7 — M.33.c.1.9 — M.32.d.7.8. — M.32.d.2.7.

   Each line when captured will be consolidated and garrisoned.

3. (a) The 50th Division will attack with two Brigades in the front line and one in Reserve.

   The 149th Infantry Brigade will be on the right and the 150th Infantry Brigade on the left, with the 151st Infantry Brigade in Reserve.

   The Boundary between the 149th Infantry Brigade and the 150th Infantry Brigade will be M.33.b.4.6 — M.33.d.0.8 — S.3.c.0.9.

   The 50th Divisional boundaries are as follows:—
   On Right (East) S.3.d.2.9 — S.3.b. Central — M.34.c.9.5. — M.34.b.5.9

On Left (West) S.2.a.6.1. – S.2.b.2.8. – M.32.d.5.0. – M.32.d.2.7.

(b) The 151st Infantry Brigade will be situated prior to zero as follows:-

    'A' Battalion — MAMETZ WOOD.
    B. Battalion — QUADRANGLE TRENCH.
    C. & D. Battalions — SHELTER WOOD area.

At zero these battalions will move:-

    A and B Battalions to O.G. 1 & 2.
    C Battalion to MAMETZ WOOD
    D Battalion to QUADRANGLE TRENCH.

The 149th and 150th Infantry Brigades will arrange for the O.G. 1 and 2 lines to be vacated at zero to allow the A. and B. Battalions 151st Infantry Brigade to occupy them.

(c) PIONEERS. The Pioneer Battalion (7th D.L.I.) will be disposed as follows:-

One Company ('B' Coy) is allotted to the 149th Infantry Brigade and one Company ('D' Coy) is allotted to the 150th Infantry Brigade and will be accommodated by them.

They will be employed making Communication trenches between the successive lines.

Infantry Brigadiers will order them forward for this work as soon as they consider the situation sufficiently favourable for the work to be carried out.

Two platoons of 'C' Coy. will be employed under the 7th Field Coy. R.E. repairing the road through S.8.d. – S.8.c. – S.8.a. – S.8.b.

They will be situated about X 23 d central at zero hour.

The Remaining half of 'C' Coy and the whole of 'A' Coy,, the Lewis Gun Detachment, Band and Details will be in reserve about X 28 b 6.9.

(d) ROYAL ENGINEERS. The 7th Field Coy. R.E. with two platoons of the Pioneer Battalion will repair the road through S.8 d. S.8 c., S.8 a, S.8 b. and will be situated at zero hour about X 23 d. central. The 1st and 2nd Northumbrian Field Coys R.E. will be in reserve about RAILWAY COPSE. They will have their technical wagons with them but not the bridging equipment.

4. WOUNDED. Wounded will be brought back as follows:—

Right Brigade. — To Advanced Collecting Posts at S.8.d.8.4. and S.8.d.8.8.

Left Brigade. — To Advanced Collecting Posts at S.8.a.1.4. and about X 12 c 9.5

At the Advanced Collecting Posts the personnel of the Field Ambulances will remove the lying down cases to the Advanced Dressing Stations at FLATIRON COPSE (S.14.c.5.2) and CONTALMAISON. Walking cases will go to CONTALMAISON.

5. STRAGGLERS. Straggler Posts will be established about S.15.a.0.9. and The CUTTING.

Stragglers will be handed over to the rearmost Battalion of the Reserve Brigade at SHELTER WOOD.

6 (a) DUMP. An advanced Divisional Dump for ammunition of all kinds except Artillery Ammunition will be established at S.14.b.1.8.

(b) An advanced R.E. Dump will be established at the end of JUTLAND ALLEY about S.2.d.9.7 and about S.14.b.9.9.

7. Officers valises and surplus mess kit will be returned to Q.M. Stores.
'B' and 'D' Coys. will send their packs to Q.M. Stores.

Transport.

Horses for Cookers and Water Carts, which will remain at Q.M. Stores will arrive at Billets at 2 o'clock to-morrow (Thursday)

'A' Company. One G.S. Wagon will be at their Billet at 2 p.m. The Wagon will convey Officers valises to Q.M. Stores and picks and shovels to Forward Billets. In addition it will dump all surplus tools at Q.M. Stores and take up 40 petrol cans and 8 Camp Kettles.
'A' Coy. will proceed in full marching order, leaving Billets at 2.15 p.m. to-morrow.

'B' Company. 2 G.S. Wagons will take up from Q.M. Stores at 2 o'clock to-morrow (Thursday) 40 petrol tins and 8 Camp Kettles to present billet and bring back Officers Valises, mens packs and surplus tools to Q.M. Stores.
'B' Coy will proceed to Forward Billets in light fighting order, carrying picks shovels, Kettles and Tins, leaving Billets after 4 p.m.

'C' Company. One G.S. Wagon detailed for 'B' Coy will call at 'C' Coy. Billet at 1 o'clock and collect all tools and Officers valises. The latter and surplus ~~valises~~ Tools will be dumped at Q.M.S. to-gether with Surplus Camp Kettles (8 per coy). This wagon will draw 40 Tins from the Stores and dump them at the dugouts at X 29 d central.
'C' Coy will arrange for party to convey half Tools, Tins and Dearies to X 28 b 6.9.
'C' Coy will leave Billets at 2.15 p.m. in full marching order.

'D' Company. 2. G.S. Wagons will be at Q.M Stores at 2 p.m. for 40 tins and 8 Camp Kettles and convey them to 'D' Coys. present Billets and bring back Officers valises, mens packs and surplus tools &c.

'D' Coy will leave for forward Billets after 4 p.m. in light fighting order, carrying tins, tools and Kettles.

Lewis Gun Detachment. The Gun Limbers will leave Q.M. Stores at 2 p.m. carrying 20 Petrol Tins, 2 Camp Kettles and proceed to the present Forward Billets.

The Detachment will leave for X 28 b 6.9 after 4 p.m. in Full Marching Order and will carry Guns, Ammunition, Tins and Kettles.

Guides. 2 Guides will be at 'A' and 'C' Coys Billets at 1.45 p.m. to guide the 1½ Coys to X 28 b 6.9 and half Company to X 23 d Central. 1. Guide will report to Lewis Gun Officer at 12 noon to conduct Guides from Detachment to X 28 b 6.9.

Rations. The Quartermaster will arrange for rations to go with transport detailed to call at the store.

Headquarters will be established as follows by 6 p.m. tomorrow.

- ADVANCED DIV. H.Q. — RAILWAY COPSE X.28 b 2.1.
- 149th INF. BRIGADE — QUARRY, S.8 b 9.1.
- 150th INF. BRIGADE — O.G.1. S.7.d.2.1.
- 151st INF. BRIGADE — MAMETZ WOOD X.24 b 9.8.
- 7th D.L.I. (Pioneers) — X 28 b 6.9.

S E C R E T.

WAR DIARY

O F

7th BATTALION D.L.I.
(PIONEERS).

Volume XIX.

OCTOBER 1916.

WAR DIARY or INTELLIGENCE SUMMARY.

7th Bn DURHAM LIGHT INFANTRY (PIONEERS)
OCTOBER 1916.
No. 19.

Army Form C. 2118.

Place	Date	Hour	Summary of Events and Information	Remarks and references to Appendices
FRICOURT	1st		C Coy continued to clear CRESCENT ALLEY as far as the junction of SPENCE TRENCH. D Coy widened and cleared SPENCE TRENCH. A Coy working on RUTHERFORD ALLEY deepened it to DURHAM TRENCH. B Coy continued work on the CONTALMAISON-MARTINPUICH road.	W.J.R.
	2nd		The Division attacked this afternoon and took the FLERS and Support Line - ridges. During the night A & D Coys under very difficult conditions succeeded in connecting up RUTHERFORD ALLEY with the final objective - on account of the barrage and congested state of the trench C Coy was unable to establish communication on the left.	W.J.R.
	3rd		C Coy connected up 26th avenue with final objective. A & D Coys attempted to complete Durham Trench but were unable to do so on account of the very heavy shelling. B Coy continued work on the roads.	W.J.R.
	4th		The Division was relieved last night by the 23rd Division and no work was done.	
	5th		This Battalion remains in the line for work on roads and tramways. D Coy worked on Tramway from S.B.B. Central. Remainder of Coys on roads.	

Army Form C: 2118.

WAR DIARY
or
INTELLIGENCE SUMMARY.
(Erase heading not required.)

Place	Date	Hour	Summary of Events and Information	Remarks and references to Appendices
FRICOURT	5th		As above.	N.T.R.
	6th		Work as above.	N.T.R.
	7th		N° 2416 Sergeant Coleman T. and N° 2566 Sergeant Davey A. were awarded the Military Medal. C Coy worked with 10.12" Field Coy R.E. on road from the CUTTING to MARTINPUICH via the CHATEAU.	N.T.R.
	8th		As above. Work in MARTINPUICH considerably hampered by enemy shelling.	N.T.R.
	9th		As above.	N.T.R.
	10th		As above. CAPTAIN M. A. Mackinnon was awarded the Military Medal. N° 1702 Pte Grant J.A. the Military Medal.	N.T.R.
	11th		Work continues as above.	N.T.R.
	12th		B Coy has taken over from D Coy the work on the railway - the Lewis gun Detachment provides various loading parties.	N.T.R.
	13th		In conjunction with the III Corps Scheme D Coy commenced work on the railway from SHELTER WOOD to MARTINPUICH. The work is chiefly ballasting & laying junctions. A Coy is working about the	N.T.R.

50

1/7 Durham L J

Vol XII

WAR DIARY
or
INTELLIGENCE SUMMARY.
(Erase heading not required.)

Army Form C. 2118.

Place	Date	Hour	Summary of Events and Information	Remarks and references to Appendices
FRICOURT	13th		Railhead preparing the ground for rails - C Coy commenced work on clearing GUN PIT Road from MARTINPUICH to main ALBERT-BAPAUME Road.	W.T.K.
	14th	9. 4.25 PM	French T. was awarded the Military Medal -	
	15th		As above	R.P.K.
	16th		Church of England Parade held at Headquarters	
	17th		As above - Work commenced this morning erecting new huts at S.13.D.8.2. by a Squad under Captain R.G. MACINTYRE	N.P.K. M.P.K.
	18th		Work as above. A Coy are now busy with the Railway running round the East of MARTINPUICH	
	19th		C Coy have cleared GUN PIT Road up to the ALBERT-BAPAUME Road.	R.P.K.
	20th		Companies worked as above.	R.P.K.
	21st		Work as above -	N.P.K.
	22nd		B Coy moved into new camp - S.13.D.8.2	M.P.K.
	23rd		C Coy engaged in filling Shell holes in GUN PIT ROAD. The	M.P.K.

WAR DIARY or INTELLIGENCE SUMMARY

Army Form C. 2118

Place	Date	Hour	Summary of Events and Information	Remarks and references to Appendices
FRICOURT	23rd		Remaining three Companies on the Railways	M.P.F.
"	24th		D Coy moved into new camp today. The following awards have been granted. Military Cross. Captain W.R. Goodrick and Captain S. Reardhead - Military Medal. No 25543 L/Sgt L.a. Bittestone and No 2284 Pte R. Maguire.	Jh.P.F.
MAMETZ	25th		The 50th Division relieved the 9th Division last night. Headquarters of this unit moved to new Camp.	M.P.F.
"	26th		Work continued as above.	
"	27th		The four Companies commenced work repairing the two main communication Trenches to the front line. A+C Coys from the SNAG TRENCH about M.17.C.4.4. towards the FLERS LINE. D+B Coys from the SNAG about M.17.D.5.6. towards the FLERS LINE via PIONEER TRENCH. Small parties continue working on new Hutments & Divisional Headquarters at SABOT COPSE.	M.P.F.
"	28th		As above. The work on left Sector is hindered by shell fire and the very bad state of the Trenches	M.P.F. M.P.F.
"	29th		Work as above. The right Sector is progressing satisfactorily.	
"	30th		A Coy moved into new Camp at S.13.D.8.2.	M.P.F.

WAR DIARY
or
INTELLIGENCE SUMMARY
(Erase heading not required.)

Army Form C. 2118

Place	Date	Hour	Summary of Events and Information	Remarks and references to Appendices
MAMETZ	31st		All companies today worked on Trenches on Left Sector - and good progress was made - Unfortunately the recent rains have caused most of the C.T.s to fall in, hampering our work considerably - W. J. Laws Captain and Adjutant, 7th Bn. Durham Light Infantry (Pioneers)	W.P.L.

SECRET.

50th Division Operation Order Number 55.

21st Sept 1916.

1. (a) On a date to be notified later (probably the 23rd Sept.) the Fourth Army will renew the attack in conjunction with the French.

   (b) The 15th Corps is to capture FACTORY CORNER and is to establish a line thence to the high ground in M.29.b.9.d. and to join up with the 3rd Corps in FLERS support line at M.29.b.4.1.

   The 1st Canadian Division will be attacking the ZOLLERN GRABEN to the North of COURCELETTE.

2. The objectives of the III Corps are shewn on the tracing already issued.

3. (a) The 50th Division will attack as its first objective the STARFISH LINE and PRUE TRENCH from M.34.b.7.8. to CRESCENT ALLEY inclusive. (M.33.b.4.6.).

   The 2nd objective will be the road from about M.28.d.8.0.- M.28.d.1.8.- M.27.d.7.4. and thence to CRESCENT ALLEY inclusive.

   The general direction of the attack is due North.

   (b) On arrival at the 2nd objective patrols must be pushed forward at once on to the best line for constructing a defensive line.

   (c) Both the STARFISH LINE and PRUE TRENCH must have parties left in them to clear out dugouts and to garrison them.

   The second objective must be consolidated as quickly as possible.

4. The 50th Division will attack with the 149th Inf. Brigade with two Battalions of the 150th Inf. Brigade attached.

   The 150th Inf. Brigade less two Battalions will be in support and the 151st Infantry Brigade in Reserve.

5. The attack will be assisted by all available artillery, details of which will be notified later, including three 2" Trench Mortars.

   The 150th Light T.M. Battery will be placed at the disposal of the 149th Inf. Brigade for the preliminary bombardment.

6. The Brigades will at zero hour be disposed as follows:—
149th Inf. Brigade and two Battalions 150th Inf. Brigade in the front line including MARTIN TRENCH, BOAST TRENCH and JACKSON TRENCH and new jump off line.
   150th Infantry Brigade — HOOK TRENCH.
   151st Infantry Brigade — 1 Battalion EYE TRENCH.
                              2 Battalions CLARKS and SWANSEA.
                              1 Battalion INTERMEDIATE LINE
All troops will be in these positions two hours before zero.

7. A Communication trench will be dug joining up PRUE TRENCH, STARFISH LINE and the jumping off trench as soon as possible.
   One Company of Pioneers is allotted to the 149th Inf. Brigade for this purpose, and will be ordered forward when the B.G.C. considers it possible for them to work.
   They will be accommodated prior to the attack by the 149th Infantry Brigade.

7a. There will be two Communication Trenches available. BETHEL SAP — RUTHERFORD ALLEY.— IN
   JUTLAND ALLEY — CRESCENT ALLEY.— OUT.

8. "C" Dump will be at junction of BETHEL SAP and CLARK'S TRENCH.
   An Engineer dump will also be formed there.

9. Headquarters will be as under:—
   Advanced Div. H.Q.   RAILWAY COPSE.
   149th Bde. H.Q.   QUARRY
   150th "   "   O.G. Line
   151st "   "   MAMETZ WOOD

           Signed H. Karslake Lt. Col.
              General Staff
                 50th Division

Issued at 8.A.M.

Pioneers,
50th Division

War Diary

1/7th Battalion Durham Light Infantry

1st-30th November 1916

(Original)

S E C R E T.

WAR DIARY

OF

7th D. L. I. (PIONEERS).

Volume No : ~~XX~~.

November 1916.

WAR DIARY or INTELLIGENCE SUMMARY

Army Form C. 2118.

7th Bn DURHAM LIGHT INFANTRY (PIONEERS)
NOVEMBER 1916
No 20.

Place	Date	Hour	Summary of Events and Information	Remarks and references to Appendices
MAMETZ	1st		B and D Coy worked on right Sector C.T. PIONEER ALLEY is cleared from the FLERS line to Battalion Headquarters in SUNKEN ROAD. C & A Coys attempted clearing PIMPLE ALLEY which is in a shocking condition. The work in new Camp torpedoes favourably with the Bandsmen. The Lewis Gun Detachments are employed on New Divisional Headquarters SABOT COPSE and small working parties.	W.T.K. W.T.K.
	2nd		A & D Coy cleared PIONEER ALLEY from SNAG to ABBAYE TRENCH.	
	3rd		The condition of PIMPLE ALLEY is so bad that A & C Corps cut a new C.T. on the left of the present one from about M.23.O.O.7. – M.23.A.1.45. – M.23.A.O.8.15 a depth of 5'. Small maintenance parties worked on PIONEER ALLEY –	W.T.K. W.T.K.
	4th		Last night the parties rested —	
	5th		Reference 50th Division Operation Order No 62 (attached) B Coy (attached to the right Sector) and C Coy + 1 Platoon from D Coy (attached left sector) took up their position in readiness in ABBAYE TRENCH and HEXHAM ROAD suffering heavy casualties before the offensive took place. CAPT. W.R. SHEPHERD was killed —	W.T.K.
	6th		As the attack failed completely on the right B Coy cleared PIONEER ALLEY which had been badly damaged by shell fire and withdrew to the FLERS LINE. C Coy made a gallant attempt to link up with the 9th Battalion but owing to a successful German Counter attack were forced to withdraw.	W.T.K.
	7th		A & D Corps trench boarded 350 yards of NEW TRENCH from FLERS LINE to PIMPLE ALLEY. C Coy came into new Camp —	W.T.K.

Army Form C. 2118.

WAR DIARY
or
INTELLIGENCE SUMMARY

(Erase heading not required.)

Instructions regarding War Diaries and Intelligence Summaries are contained in F. S. Regs., Part II. and the Staff Manual respectively. Title Pages will be prepared in manuscript.

Place	Date	Hour	Summary of Events and Information	Remarks and references to Appendices
MAMETZ	8	—	All Coys prepared overland route alongside RUTHERFORD ALLEY utilising its trench Boards in the C.T. Work continues in Camp erecting huts.	W.P.L.
	9		A B & C Coys cut new C.T. from about M.23.A.0.6½ to M.170.3½.3½ to an average depth of 5'. D Coy cleared PIONEER ALLEY from FLERS LINE to its first SUNKEN ROAD. The C.T's are in a very bad state on account of the rain.	D.P.L.
	10		A & C Coys continue work on new C.T. with a view to revetting – owing to numerous falls they were unable to make much progress revetting but completed the trench in revetments – B and D Coys worked on PIONEER ALLEY	W.P.L. D.P.L.
	11		Work as above.	W.P.L.
	12		As above. The Corps continue to revet the C.T.s. Work is hampered by heavy shelling & having to clear breaches and falls as above.	W.P.L. W.P.L. D.P.L.
	13		The Corps worked as above.	
	14		Trenches are continually falling in requiring a great amount of labour clearing them.	
	15			
	16		A Coy cut a small deviation from PIONEER ALLEY near HEXHAM ROAD. Aviation's are very bad parts of the trench.	D.P.L.
	17		The Divn is in is being relieved by the 1st Division	W.P.L.
	18		We took over repair of road S.14.B.8.9 – S.8.A.8.6 from 6th Welch (Pioneers)	W.P.L.

2449 Wt. W14957/M90 750,000 1/16 J.B.C. & A. Forms/C.2118/12.

WAR DIARY or INTELLIGENCE SUMMARY

Army Form C. 2118.

Place	Date	Hour	Summary of Events and Information	Remarks and references to Appendices
MAMETZ	19th		Work commenced on road today with three Corps. The Hunts Coy being employed on work in Camp. The work consists in clearing the banks of road from its side of the road, levelling and cutting drains.	W.T.K.
	20th		4.6 Lewis Gunners employed in erecting NISSEN HUTS in BAZENTIN-LE-PETIT. Our transport employed in carrying road metal.	W.T.K. W.T.K.
	21st		Work as above.	
	22nd		As above. A party from A Coy is employed in laying light railway from road to Dressing Station and also repairing its Dug outs.	W.T.K. W.T.K.
	23rd		Work continued as above.	
	24th		As above. Party from C Coy commenced work on Camp at N.E. end of BAZENTIN-LE-PETIT VILLAGE.	
	25th			
	26th			
	27th		as above	W.T.K.
	28th			
	29th			
	30th			

W. T. Lewis
Captain
7. 3rd Durham Lt Infy.

SECRET
Copy No 6.

50th Division Operation Order No 62.

Reference
Trench map. 1/10,000.   3rd November 1916.

1. 50th Division Operation Order No 60 is cancelled.

2 (a)   The 50th Division of the III Corps, and 1st Anzac Corps are attacking the GIRD LINE as far west as the BAPAUME road, on November 5th.

(b)   A Brigade of the 2nd Australian Division will be on the immediate right of the 50th Division.

(c)   The 48th Division on the left of 50th Division is not attacking, but is assisting the attack of the 50th Division by Artillery and machine gun fire.

3.   The 50th Division will capture the GIRD LINE and GIRD SUPPORT LINE from M.12.c.2.9. as far north as an E. and W. line through M.17.a.5.8 including the BUTTE and the QUARRY M.17.a.0.6.

4. (a)   The attack will be carried out by the 151st Infantry Brigade with two battalions of the 149th Infantry Brigade attached.
    H.Q of the Brigade M.22.d.6.2.

(b)   The 149th Infantry Brigade less two battalions will be in support in the STARFISH LINE, PRUE TRENCH and FLERS SWITCH.
    H.Q. of the Brigade at the COUGH DROP

(c)   The 150th Infantry Brigade will be in reserve with two Battalions

South of HIGH WOOD, and two Battalions in MAMETZ WOOD.

H.Q. of the Brigade BAZENTIN LE GRAND.

The 149th and 150th Infantry Brigades will be in their final positions by 6.A.M on the morning of the attack, and will show themselves as little as possible.

The two Battalions of the 150th Infantry Brigade* to move to HIGH WOOD, will move at zero.

5(a). The attack will be supported by all the available artillery.

(b). An intense barrage will start at zero 200 yards in front of our front trenches.

This barrage will lift at zero ~~plus (four)~~ minutes and will creep back at 50 yards per minute till it reaches a line 300 yards beyond the GIRD SUPPORT LINE, when it will be reduced to a light barrage.

At zero plus 30 (thirty) minutes all the Divisional Artillery guns will cease except the forward batteries which will continue to fire steadily on COUPE TRENCH.

The remainder of the artillery will be ready to put on a barrage 200 yards beyond the GIRD SUPPORT LINE in case of necessity.

5.(c) There are two points in the German front line which are too close to our line for the barrage to be effective, viz:-

M.17. d. 6. 8.
M.17. a. 4. 3.

These two points and a portion of the trench in the neighbourhood of them must be bombarded with Light Trench Mortars

3) under arrangements to be made by the B.G.C. 151st Brigade.

(d) Detailed Artillery Programmes have been issued to all concerned.

(e) Two Medium T.M. Batteries will take part in the bombardment, one on either flank, and are put at the disposal of the B.G.C. 151st Infantry Brigade.

6. (a) The objective when captured will be consolidated and will be held by as few men as possible.

(b) If necessary parties must be prepared to work outwards on gaining their objectives to gain touch with neighbouring units and to assist them if necessary to gain their objectives.

(c) The objective is to be connected up with the present front line as soon as possible after it is captured.

For this purpose two Companies of Pioneers are allotted to 151st Infantry Brigade.

They will make the following C.T's:-
M.17.d.5.6. — M.17.d.6.8.
M.17.a.4.0. — M.17.a.4.3.

These Companies will be put on to this work as soon as the B.G.C. considers conditions are favourable.

7. The 7th D.L.I. (Pioneers), less two companies and the three Field Companies will be employed under the C.R.E. to whom separate instructions have been issued.

8. All Officers and N.C.O's will carry flares and will light them when called upon to do so by the Contact Patrol.

All forward posts must be specially warned to light flares.

9. A scheme for the various means of communication has been issued to all concerned.

4/

10. <u>Advanced Dressing Posts</u> will be established at
    THE QUARRY. — M.22.d.3.2.
    SEVEN ELMS. — M.28.d.6.3.

<u>Divisional Collecting Station</u>
    BAZENTIN LE GRAND — S.9.c.6.1.

<u>Advanced Dressing Station</u>
    BAZENTIN LE PETIT.

11. The Reserve Brigade will detail two parties of one Officer and 10 men each to be at M.29.a.2.3. and M.22.d.3.5., to take over Prisoners and conduct them to the Corps Cage at BAZENTIN LE PETIT.

12. An Advanced Divisional Dump for Grenades, etc, and R.E. material will be established about M.23.d.3.9.

13. Zero hour will be notified later. 9.10 a.m.

14. Reports to 50th Division Advanced H.Q. at BAZENTIN LE GRAND WOOD, S.14.d.1.7.

Signed H. Karslake.
General Staff, Lt. Col.
50th Division

3rd November. 1916.
Issued at 2-15 pm.

SECRET.
Copy No.
50th Division
G.X. 2868/12.

Re 50th Division O.O. No 60.

1. The attack will probably take place on the 2nd November.

2. The objective has been slightly altered and is now the GIRD LINE as far north as an E and W line through M.17.a.5.8 as shown on the attached sketch map.*

3. The 15th Division will not attack on our left, but the 14th Infantry Brigade 5th Australian Division, will attack on our right, as previously arranged.

   The artillery of the 15th Division will assist to protect our left flank. It is going to carry out its original programme up to zero plus 30 minutes.

   After that time it is going to keep a steady fire on the GALLWITZ SWITCH about M.10.a.2.6 to M.3.d.8.0. to keep down Machine Gun fire.

4. Zero hour will be 8-0.A.M.

5. One Officer per Artillery Brigade and Infantry Brigade will meet a Staff Officer of the Division at the Brigade H.Q. BAZENTIN LE GRAND at 6. p.m. on 1st November to synchronise watches.

31st October 1916.

* Issued to:- 149 Inf. Brigade
    150 "   "
    151 "   "
    C.R.A Right Div Group
    15th Div
    5th Australian Division

(Signed.) H. Karslake. Lt. Col.
General Staff
50th Division

Secret

Copy No 6

50th DIVISION OPERATION ORDER No. 60.

REF. 1/10,000 trench map.   26th October 1916

Issued to:
149th Inf. Bde.
150 " "
151 " "

1. (a) The Fourth Army is continuing the attack on the 30th instant; the objective is shewn on the attached tracing. *

   (b) The 14th Infantry Brigade (H.Q. M.30.c.3.1) 5th Australian Division is attacking on the right of the 50th Division.

   The 44 Inf. Bgde. (H.Q. M.33.a.1.9) 15th Division is attacking on the left of the 50th Division.

   (c) The 15th Division is going to push patrols across the VALLEY if the situation admits.

   (d) Should the wind be S.W. on the 30th, the 15th Division is going to form a smoke barrage on the line M.17.a.1½.5 – M.10.d.9.3.

   The barrage will start at zero, and will be clear at plus 6 minutes.

2. The 50th Division will capture the GIRD LINE and GIRD SUPPORT LINE from M.18.c.2.8½. to the road at M.10.d.9.2½. and will push patrols forward to gain touch with the enemy, paying particular attention to the LE BARQUE SWITCH and WARLENCOURT.

3. The attack will be carried out by:-
   149th Inf. Bde. on the right.   H.Q. The COUGH DROP.
   150th Inf. Bde. on the left.   H.Q. M.22.d.6.2.

   The boundary between Brigades is shown on the attached tracing *

   The 151st Inf. Bde. will be in reserve.   H.Q. BAZENTIN LE GRAND.
   2 battalions at HIGH WOOD.
   2 battalions at BAZENTIN LE PETIT.

   All troops to be in position two hours before zero.

4. The attack will be supported by all the available artillery. An intense barrage will start at zero 200 yards in front of our front line and will creep back at 50 yards per minute, halting on a line about 300 yards beyond the GIRD SUPPORT LINE.

2nd sheet.

A detailed programme will be issued to all concerned.

5. The attack will be assisted by two TANKS one on each flank of the Division.

Detailed instructions for these TANKS have been issued to all concerned.

6 (a) The objective when captured will be consolidated and will be held with as few men as possible.

(b) If necessary Brigades will on reaching their objectives work outwards so as to assist neighbouring formations to get forward.

Touch must be gained all along the line.

(c) The new objective is to be connected up with SNAG TRENCH as soon as possible after it is captured.

For this purpose one Pioneer Company is allotted to each of the attacking Brigades to make the following C.Ts: as under:—

B Coy. with 14g th Inf. Bde. from M.17.d.5.6. — M.17.d.6.8.
C Coy. with 150 th Inf. Bde. from M.17.c.0.9. — M.17.a.0.6. and thence by the BUTTE to M.17.a.4.7.

These Companies will be put on to this work as soon as Brigadiers consider conditions are favourable for work.

7. PIONEERS and R.E. The 7th D.L.I. (Pioneers) less two Companies and the three Field Companies R.E. will be employed under the C.R.E. to whom separate instructions have been issued.

8. CONTACT PATROLS. All Officers and N.C.Os. will carry flares, and will light them when called upon to do so by the Contact Patrol.

All forward posts must be especially warned to light flares.

9. COMMUNICATION. A scheme for visual signalling is to be prepared beforehand by Brigades.

10. MEDICAL. Advanced Dressing Posts will be established at

THE QUARRY . M.22.d.3.2.
SEVEN ELMS M.28.d.6.3.

Divisional Collecting Station:- BAZENTIN LE GRAND S.9.c.6.1.
Advanced Dressing Station :- BAZENTIN LE PETIT.

Sheet 3.

11. PRISONERS. The Reserve Brigade will detail two parties of one Officer and 10 men each to be at M.29.a.2.3 and M.22.d.2.5 to take over prisoners and conduct them to the Corps Cage at BAZENTIN LE PETIT.

12. DUMP An Advanced Divisional Dump for grenades etc. and R.E. material will be established at about M.23.d.3.9.

13. REPORTS. Reports to 50th Div. Advanced H.Q. at SABOT COPSE per this office.

(Sgd) W. F. Laing,
Capt. & Adjutant,
7th. D.L.I. (Pioneers)

SECRET.
Copy No 6.
50th Division
G.X. 2868./6.

re 50th Division O.O. No 60. para H.

An intense artillery barrage will commence at zero hour on a line 200 yards in front of our leading jumping off trench.

At zero plus 3 minutes it will move forward at 50 yards per minute till it reaches a line 300 yards beyond the GIRD SUPPORT line, when it will be reduced to a light barrage.

At zero plus 30 minutes all guns will cease except the forward batteries which will continue to fire steadily on COUPE TRENCH.

This will enable patrols to go forward if the situation admits of it.

The remainder of the artillery will be ready to put on a barrage 200 yards beyond the GIRD SUPPORT line in case of necessity.

The position of the German line from M.17.d.6.8. to a point about 150 yards North West of it must be barraged by Light & Medium trench mortars at zero hour, as it is too close to our front line for the Artillery to fire on with safety.

This barrage and the details of the lift will be arranged by the B.G.C. 149. Inf. Brigade to suit his attack.

Sgd. H. Karslake. Lt. Col.
General Staff
50th Division

30th October 1916

G.X.2868/4.

The Operation mentioned in 50th Division Operation Order No 60 dated 26th October 1916. is again postponed two days, and will take place on Friday 3rd November instead of 28th October.

Sgd. H Karslake Lt.Col.
General Staff
50th Division

31st October 1916

SECRET.

WAR DIARY

OF

7th BATTALION DURHAM LIGHT INFANTRY (PIONEERS).

Volume ~~XXI~~.

December 1916.

WAR DIARY — 7th Bn DURHAM LIGHT INFANTRY (PIONEERS)
INTELLIGENCE SUMMARY — DECEMBER No 21.
Army Form C. 2118.

Place	Date	Hour	Summary of Events and Information	Remarks and references to Appendices
MAMETZ	1st	—	A.B.& D. Companies continue work on the BAZENTIN ROAD S.14.B.8.9 - S.8.A.8.6. The road is very narrow and requires a great deal of labour throwing back the earth to enable a drain to be cut and allow 23' access - C Coy are engaged in erecting a camp at Site 4 - S.8.B.2.6.	
	2nd		Church of England Parade Service held in Camp -	W.J.L.
	3rd		Work continued as above - The road as far as the FORK ROADS bends the Church is practically completed. Requiring only an unlimited supply of metal - C Coy continue work on huts -	W.J.L.
	4th			
	5th			
	6th			W.J.L.
	7th			
	8th			
	9th			
	10th		Church of England Parade Service held in Camp -	W.J.L.
	11th		Work continued as above. A Coy took over work on the HIGH WOOD ROAD from S.8.A.8.6 — S.8.C.1.2. The road is in an extremely bad condition and the earth has to be thrown back from feet at the sides - A Natural drain has been unearthed in the westside of the BAZENTIN ROAD and a pavement at the East side - constantly benefiting infantry parties -	
	17th		Church of England Parade Service held in Camp -	W.J.L.
				W.J.L.

1.

WAR DIARY
or
INTELLIGENCE SUMMARY

7th Bn DURHAM LIGHT INFANTRY (PIONEERS)
DECEMBER No 21.
Army Form C. 2118.

Place	Date	Hour	Summary of Events and Information	Remarks and references to Appendices
MAMETZ	1st	—	A, B & D Companies continue work on the BAZENTIN ROAD S.14.B.6.9-S.8.A.8.6. The road is very narrow and requires a great deal of labour throwing out earth to enable a drain to be cut and allow 23' across. C Coy are engaged in erecting a camp at Site 4.- S.8.B.2.6.	W.J.R.
	2nd		Church of England Parade Service held in Camp.	W.J.R.
	3rd		Work continued as above. The road as far as the FORK ROADS beyond the Church is practically completed, requiring only an occasional polish. C Coy continue work on huts.	W.J.R.
	4th			
	5th			
	6th			W.J.R.
	7th			
	8th			
	9th		Church of England Parade Service held in Camp.	W.J.R.
	10th			
	11th to 16th		Work continued as above. A Coy took over work on the HIGH WOOD ROAD from S.8.A.9.6 - S.8.C.1.2. The road is in an extremely bad condition and the earth has to be thrown back four feet at the sides. A natural drain has been unearthed in the West verge of the BAZENTIN ROAD and a pavement at the East side — considerably benefiting infantry parties.	W.J.R.
	17th		Church of England Parade Service held in Camp.	W.J.R.

Army Form C. 2118.

WAR DIARY
or
INTELLIGENCE SUMMARY

(Erase heading not required.)

Instructions regarding War Diaries and Intelligence Summaries are contained in F. S. Regs., Part II. and the Staff Manual respectively. Title Pages will be prepared in manuscript.

Place	Date	Hour	Summary of Events and Information	Remarks and references to Appendices
NAME 72	18th to 24th		Work continued as above – The land at Site 4 has been completed. An – Work progressed favourably on the ROADS. The work is somewhat hampered by lack of road-metal –	W.J.L.
	25th		Christmas was considered a holiday. Inter-Company football matches in the morning and afternoon, and concerts in the evening.	W.J.L.
	26th to 30th		The Road upon which this unit has worked at sections from S.14.B.8.9 – S.8.C.1.2 has been finished during this week with the exception of the repair of the surface which requires more transport than we are able to supply – See	W.J.L.
	31st		Opm.Sg.59. Division letter attached. Church of England Service held in Camp –	W.J.L.

W. D. Sparrow
Captain & adjutant
7 Bn Durham L.I. Infty
(Pioneers)

NDRE/

Herewith extract from 50th Div/G.X. 3155 d/26/12/16.

" The Corps Commander, Sir W. PULTENEY, K.C.B.,
D.S.O., visited each Brigade on the 5th and
6th December and thanked them for the good
work they had done since they arrived in the
Corps at the beginning of August.

Not only did he thank them for the good work
done in action, but also for the equally
important work on roads and railways, which
made offensive operations possible.

He remarked that it was not until he had seen
the areas of the other Corps in the Fourth
Army when acting as Army Commander that he
realised fully what magnificent work had been
done by the 50th Division. "

           SGD. H. KARSLAKE, Lt.Col.

26:12:16.   General Staff, 50th Division.

       2.

I think you will be glad to know this.

          Sgd. E. HENDERSON, Major R.E.
27:12:16.   C.R.E. 50th Division.

Belfat
Sector

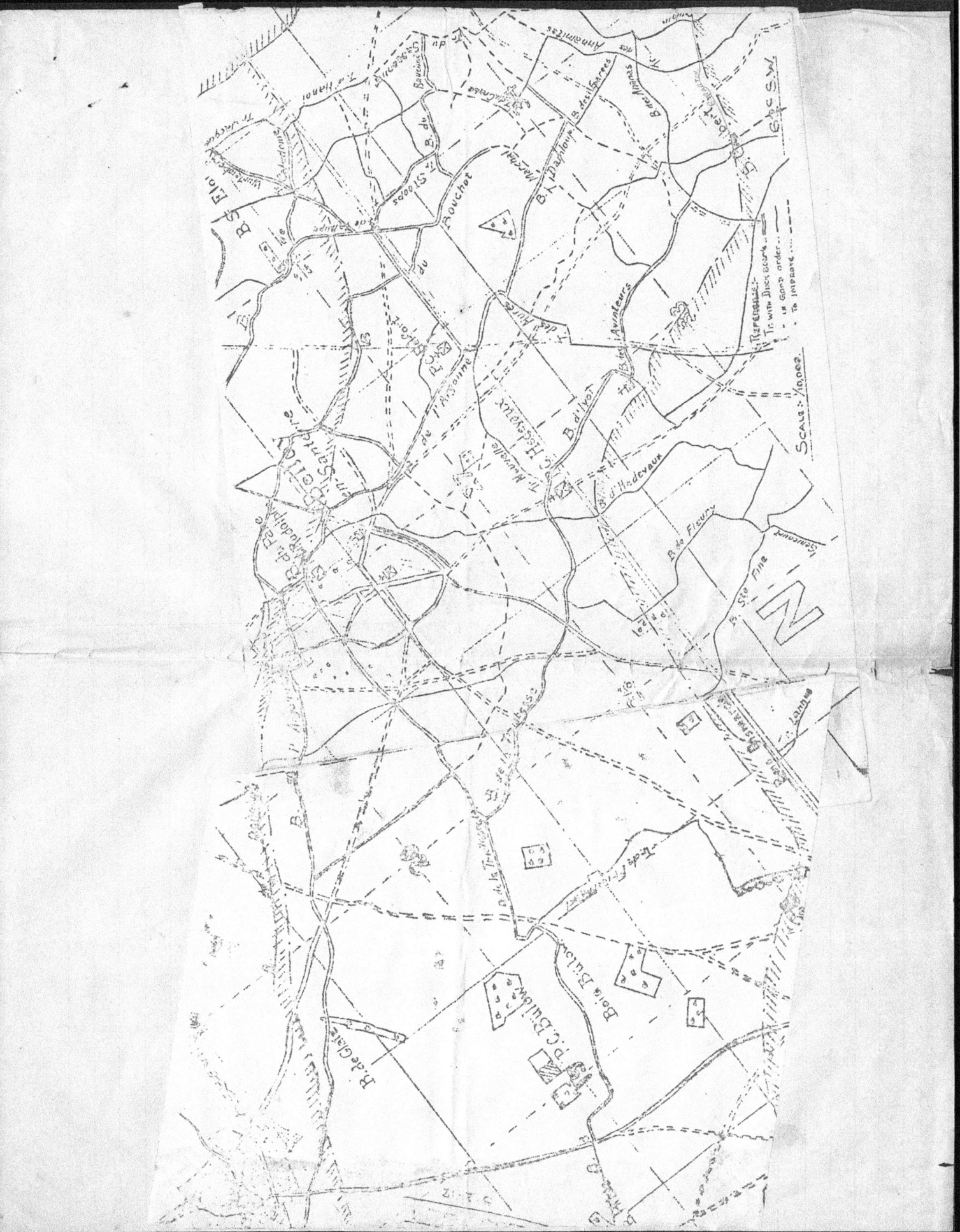

Original.

SECRET.

WAR DIARY

OF

7th Battalion D.L.I. (Pioneers).

Volume No: XXII.
****

January, 1917.

WAR DIARY or INTELLIGENCE SUMMARY

Army Form C. 2118.

7th Bn DURHAM LIGHT INFANTRY PIONEERS

JANUARY 1917. No 22

(Erase heading not required.)

Instructions regarding War Diaries and Intelligence Summaries are contained in F. S. Regs., Part II. and the Staff Manual respectively. Title Pages will be prepared in manuscript.

Place	Date	Hour	Summary of Events and Information	Remarks and references to Appendices
MAMETZ	1st		A and B Coys commenced work on PIONEER ALLEY. C Coy on TURK LANE and D Coy on FACTORY AVENUE. The trenches are in a very bad state and work consists in cleaning, draining and revetting with "U" frames and expanded metal.	S.F.K.
	2nd 3rd 4th 5th 6th 7th		Work continued as above. Progress made is somewhat slow on account of the bad condition of the trench.	L.J.K.
	8th		C Coy gave up work on TURK LANE and assisted D Coy on FACTORY AVENUE	R.Sm
	9th		Work as above. The Lewis Gun Detachment are engaged in repairing the overland tracks.	R.Sm
	10th 11th 12th		Work continued as above.	R.Sm
	13th 14th		A and B Coys continue work on PIONEER ALLEY. C and D Coys " " on FACTORY AVENUE. The Lewis Gun Detachment are engaged in keeping overland routes in repair.	R.Sm

WAR DIARY
or
INTELLIGENCE SUMMARY
(Erase heading not required.)

7th BATT: Durham Light Infantry (Pioneers)
Army Form C. 2118.
January, 1917.

Place	Date	Hour	Summary of Events and Information	Remarks and references to Appendices
A	15th		Work continued on PIONEER ALLEY by A and B Coys. FACTORY AVENUE by C and D Coys. OVERLAND ROUTE by Lewis Gun Detachment.	
	16			
	17			
	18			
	19			R.M.
	20			
	21			
	22		The work during this period was greatly hampered by bad weather conditions.	
	23			
	24			
	25			R.M.
	26		A way is made clear between the FLERS and 250 yards West of the BLUE CUT ROAD. Work ceases on the night of the 26th.	
	27			
	28			
	29			R.M.
	30		Battalion training carried on.	
	31		Battalion proceeds to near Bresle.	R.M.

7th Bn DURHAM LIGHT INFANTRY (PIONEERS) Army Form C.2118.

FEBRUARY 1917

WAR DIARY
or
INTELLIGENCE SUMMARY
(Erase heading not required.)

Place	Date	Hour	Summary of Events and Information	Remarks and references to Appendices
BTN HQRS	1st		Owing to the severe frost training was in practice 6 mile route marches were arranged and carried out daily.	A.L.G.
	9th			
HAMEL	10th		The Battalion marched to HAMEL [62D. P.10.c.]	A.L.G.
	11th		Church of England Parade Service held at HAMEL	A.L.G. A.L.G.
BOIS St MARTIN	12th		Battalion marched to SOUTH CAMP BOIS St MARTIN (R.29.C.)	
	13th		Battalion employed on work in new Camp.	A.L.G.
	14th		A Coy moved to Dug-outs in BERNY [62c.T.2] and B Coy to Dug outs in BELLOY [62c.N.27]. The former working on BOYAU VIII BIS C.T. and the latter on TRISTESSE C.T. The remainder of the Battalion carried out work in Camp, in Division al area namely erection of latrines, bathhouses, Divisional Baths, erection of NISSEN HUTS and Prisoners of War cage.	A.L.G.
	15th to		as above - The Lewis Gun Detachment moved to advanced area SATYRE COPSE (R.29.c. central) for work on BOYAU III BIS.	A.L.G.
	18th			
	19th		(R.29.c. central) for work on BOYAU III BIS. One Platoon from D coy proceeded to Dug outs in ESTREES (M.30.c. central) to assist A.Coy.	A.L.G.
	20th		One Platoon from D Coy proceeded to Dug outs in ASSEVILLERS. Road about M.21.a.5.2.	A.L.G.

Army Form C. 2118.

WAR DIARY
or
INTELLIGENCE SUMMARY
(Erase heading not required.)

Instructions regarding War Diaries and Intelligence Summaries are contained in F. S. Regs., Part II. and the Staff Manual respectively. Title Pages will be prepared in manuscript.

Place	Date	Hour	Summary of Events and Information	Remarks and references to Appendices
BOIS S.T MARTIN	21st		Work continues as before - the O.T.S. are falling in very quickly on account of the thaw.	A.P.
	22nd to 25th		as above. Work carried on Camps.	A.P.Q.
	26th to 28th		Satisfactory progress made in CAMPS and O.T.S.	A.P.R.

J. T. Young

Captain and Adjutant/for Officer
Commanding 7th Bn. Durham Light Infantry (Pioneers).

Vol 23

SECRET

War·Diary
of
7th Battn D·L·I (Pioneers)
Volumn XXIV

March·1917

WAR DIARY
or
INTELLIGENCE SUMMARY

Army Form C.2118.

7th Bn DURHAM LIGHT INFANTRY (PIONEERS)
MARCH 1917
No. 24

Place	Date	Hour	Summary of Events and Information	Remarks and references to Appendices
BOIS S? MARTIN	1st		A Coy continued work on right sector - Namely maintenance of BOYAU IV BIS and BOYAU II BIS. - B Coy on the left sector maintained BOYAU DE LA TRISTESSE.	MAPS ANNEXED N.T.R.
	2nd		Work continued as above. The Lewis Gun detachment engaged in chaining round thoroughf ESTREES. and remainder of Battalion engaged on work in camps at FEUCAUCOURT and thoroughfart Divisional area.	N.T.R.
	3rd 4th 5th 6th 7th		Work continued as above - The work on the forward C.Ts has been exceptionally good.	N.T.R.
	8th		The Battalion concentrated in BOIS S? MARTIN. [62.D.R.29.B. central]	N.T.R.
MORCOURT	9th 10th		The Battalion marched to MORCOURT [62.D.Q.16] (See Operation orders No 3) These days were spent cleaning up and Squad Drill	N.T.R. N.T.R.
	11th 12th			
	13th		C and D Coys proceeded to VILLERS-BRETONNEUX [62.D.O.29] for work under the IIIrd Corps - See Operation orders No 3	N.T.R.
	14th		The Rifle Band proceeded to VILLERS-BRETONNEUX. Work commenced by	

Army Form C. 2118.

WAR DIARY
or
INTELLIGENCE SUMMARY
(Erase heading not required.)

Instructions regarding War Diaries and Intelligence Summaries are contained in F. S. Regs., Part II. and the Staff Manual respectively. Title Pages will be prepared in manuscript.

Place	Date	Hour	Summary of Events and Information	Remarks and references to Appendices
ORCOURT	14.		Three two Companies in hacking furnaces in BOIS DE BLAGNY [N.36] and in existing Railway Siding at BLAGNY STATION.	W.P.K.
	15.		As above. The remainder of Battalion continued Company training and improving camps and rifle ranges in the area.	W.P.K
	16 to 24		As above. The work done by C and D Coys has been exceptionally good.	W.P.K
	25.		H and B Companies relieved C and D Coys - see Operation Orders No 4 attached.	W.P.K.
	26 to 29		As above	W.P.K.
	30.		Battalion moved to LA HOUSSOYE [I.3.] See Operation Orders No 5	W.P.K.
	31.		Battalion moved to TALMAS. See Operation Orders No 6	W.P.K

W. P. Kaung
Captain and adjutant

7th Bn. Durham L.I. Pioneers.   SECRET.

OPERATION ORDERS No 8.   8:3:17.

1. The Battalion will move to BOUQUEMAISON to-morrow and will parade at 9-10.a.m. in MAIN STREET in the following order:- Signallers, "B" Coy, "C" Coy, Div and Bn Band, "D" Coy, "A" Coy, Lewis Gun Detachment, "A" Echelon Transport, "B" Echelon Transport, Headquarters Details, with the head of the column opposite the Orderly Room facing N.

2. Blankets in bundles of 10 will be taken to Q.M.Stores by 8.a.m.
"A" Coy will provide a loading party of 1 N.C.O. and 6 men (unfit for marching). These men will travel with the wagon if possible.

3. Officers valises and Mess kit will be ready for collection at 8.a.m.

4. Maltese cart, Cookers and Dixies will be collected at 8-30.a.m.

5. Companies will march closed up.

6. Divisional time will be sent round at 7-30.a.m.

(Sgd) W. F. Laing.
Capt. & Adjutant.

7th Bn. Durham Light Infantry, Pioneers.   SECRET.

OPERATION ORDER No 1.

1. The Battalion will move to MORCOURT on the 9th inst.

2. Reveille 5-30.a.m.

3. Breakfast 6-0.a.m.

4. All blankets (in bundles of 10 and labelled) Band boxes, and Supplies, will be at Q.M.Stores ready for placing on lorries at 7-45.a.m.

5. Officers Valises and Mess baskets will be at Q.M.Stores at 8-30.a.m. The Transport Officer will arrange for Baggage wagons, Mess cart, and Headquarters limber to be there at that time.

6. All K Tool carts, Lewis Gun Limbers and handcarts will be packed on Transport lines before 5-0.p.m. on 8th inst.

7. The Battalion will rendezvous on the main AMIENS-ESTREES road at 9-20.a.m. in the following order:- Signallers. Bugle Band, and Divisional Band, "D", "C", "B", "A" Coys, Lewis Gun Detachment, Rear of the column to be West of the Q.M.Stores. All Headquarters details will march with their Companies. Coy Storemen will report to Transport Officer on arrival at MORCOURT. One cook per company will march with cook engine. Other cooks and spare Transport men will march in the rear of the 2nd Line Transport in charge of Sgt Hull.

8. All maps of present area will be handed in to Orderly Room by 4-0.p.m. on 8th inst.

9. Strict attention will be paid to march discipline. 100 yards interval will be observed between companies.

10. All huts, horse lines and surroundings will be left clean.

(Sgd) W.F.Laing
Capt. & Adjutant.
7 th. Bn. D.L.I. Pioneers

7th D.L.I. Pioneers.

OPERATION ORDERS.   No 3.   SECRET.

1. "C" and "D" Coys in charge of Capt. M.E.Mail will proceed to VILLERS - BRETONNEUX via WARFUSÉE on the 13th inst.

2. The party will rendezvous in RUE DE PERONNE at 9-20.a.m. with the head of the column at the Four Roads Q.16.central ready to move off at 9-30.a.m.

3. The following will accompany the party:-
    - 2. Chargers
    - 4. Tool wagons
    - 1. Water cart
    - 2. Cook engines.

   The horses of the tool wagons and cook engines will return to Headquarters as soon as possible after the arrival of the party.

4. All blankets in bundles of ten and labelled will be at the Quarter Masters Store at 8-0.a.m.

   O.C.Coys will detail 1 Officer, 1 N.C.O. and 3 men to be ready at Q.M.Stores at 8-0.a.m. These will accompany the wagon.

   One Officer and 20 other ranks from "D"Coy will report to Camp Commandant, 111 Corps, VILLERS-BRETONNEUX at 10-0.a.m. on the 13th inst to act as billeting party. O.C.Detachment will report to C.E. 111 Corps on arrival at destination for instructions, and to this Office, that relief has been completed. For this purpose two cyclist orderlies will accompany the party.

   Rations for the 14th inst, and Officers' valises will leave Q.M.Stores at 2-0.p.m.

   A guard of 1 N.C.O. and 2 men from "D"Coy will accompany these wagons.

   The detachment will be rationed after the 14th inst, under Corps arrangements.

   All detached parties must be in possession of written instructions.

(Sgd) R.G.Macintyre, Capt.
for Capt. & Adjutant.
7th D.L.I. Pioneers.

12:3:17.

7th Bn. Durham. L.I. Pioneers.

OPERATION ORDERS No 4.

1.　　On Sunday 25th inst "A" and "B" Coys will proceed to VILLERS BRETONNEUX and "C" and "D" Coys will return to MORCOURT. Time of departure 2-15.p.m.

2.　　1 Officer from "B" Coy, 1 Officer and 3 N.C.Os from "C" Coy and 1 Officer and 3 N.C.Os from "D" Coy will remain behind until Tuesday morning to assist in the handing over of the work.

3.　　An advance party of 1 Officer and 10 men from "C" Coy and 1 Officer and 10 men from "A" Coy will leave billets at 10.a.m. and take over new billets, and prepare tea.

4.　　1 Motor lorry will be at Q"M"Stores at 8.a.m. "A" and "B" Coys blankets in bundles of 10 will be ready at that time for loading, "A" Coy will provide 2 men to proceed with the lorry, "C" and "D" Coys blankets will be ready for loading outside of billets at 9.a.m. "C" Coy will detail 2 men to return with the lorry.

5.　　The Bugle band will remain at VILLERS BRETONNEUX. It will accompany "C" and "D" Coys until "A" and "B" Coys meet on the march when it will return to VILLERS BRETONNEUX.

6.　　Coys will pay particular attention to march discipline (vide Corps Commanders notes).

7.　　1 G.S.Wagon with Officer's valises and mess kit will proceed with both parties. The wagon from VILLERS BRETONNEUX remaining at MORCOURT and the wagon from MORCOURT remaining at VILLERS BRETONNEUX. Valises and mess kit will be ready for loading at 1-45.p.m.

8.　　Cookers.
　　　　"A" Coy will take over "D"Coy's.
　　　　"D" Coy will take over "A" "
　　　　"B" Coys cooker will proceed to VILLERS BRETONNEUX.

　　　　　　　　　　　　　　(Sgd) W. F. Laing.
　　　　　　　　　　　　　　　　Capt. & Adjutant.

24:3:17.

SECRET.

7th Durham Light Infantry, Pioneers.   29:3:17.

OPERATION ORDERS No 5.

1. The Battalion will move to LA HOUSSOYE to-morrow via VILLERS BRETONNEUX - CORBIE - LANEUILLE.
   Headquarters and "C" and "D" Coys will parade in the Village to-morrow morning at 8-30.a.m.in the following order:- Signallers, Div.Band, "C" Coy, "D" Coy, Lewis Gun Detachment, "A" Echelon Transport, "B" Echelon Transport.
   Head of the column will be opposite billet No 89 facing N.W.

2. Detachment at VILLERS-BRETONNEUX will be clear of the main road ready to join the Battalion as it marches through the Village at 10-0.a.m.

3. Blankets in bundles of 10, and 5 Officers valises from "C" Coy will be at the Q.M.Stores at 6-30.a.m. Two G.S.Wagons with 100 blankets, 5 Officers valises, rations and crates for cookers, and water carts with Detachment will leave MORCOURT for VILLERS-BRETONNEUX at 7-0.a.m. The Transport Officer will arrange for the fixing of the crates. Blankets, valises, and Mess kit belonging to Detachment will be loaded on the wagons as soon as the wagons arrive.

4. Maltese cart horses for cooker and G.S.Wagon will collect dixies etc at 6-0.a.m.

5. The Bugle band will join the Divisional band at VILLERS-Bretonneux.

6. Every boot must be dubbined and socks slightly soaped.

7. No man will fall out without written permission from an Officer. O.C.Coys will take steps to prepare chits in readiness.

8. No water will be drunk on the line of march without permission from an Officer.

9. Usual intervals will be maintained between Coys- 100 yards will be maintained between every twelve wagons.

10. Billets will be left clean, O.C.Detachment will obtain a certificate to this effect.

11. Remainder of Officers valises, Mess kit etc will be ready for collection at 7-45.a.m.

                                        (Sgd) W. F. Laing.
                                              Capt. & Adjutant.

7th Bn Durham Lt. Infty. Pioneers

OPERATION ORDERS   No. 6.   SECRET   30-3-17

1. The Battalion will move to TALMAS (Sheet 57.D S.3.) via MOLLIENS au BOIS and VILLERS-BOCAGE and will parade on main AMIENS-BAPAUME road at 8-30.AM. in the following order:- Signallers, Div. Band, "C" Coy, "D" Coy, Bugle Band, "B" Coy, "A" Coy, Lewis Gun Detachment, "A" Echelon Transport, "B" Echelon Transport, Headquarters Details, with the head of the column at the Cross Roads at the west end of the Village.

2. Blankets in bundles of 10 will be ready at the Q.M. Stores at 7-0.AM.

    Officer's valises & Mess kit will be ready for collection at 7-45.AM.

    1 N.C.O. & 3 men from both "A" Coy and "B" Coy will report to the Q.M. at 7-0.AM to act as loading party.

3. Maltese cart, cookers & Dixies will be collected at 7-45.AM.

4. Usual precautions will be taken to prevent sore feet.

5. As the amount of Transport has been considerably reduced every endeavour must be made by all ranks to make the loads as light as possible.

6. Haversack rations will be carried

(Sgd) W. F. Laing
Capt. & Adjutant
7 D.L.I
Pioneers

Army Form C. 2118.

7th DURHAM LIGHT INFANTRY (PIONEERS) WAR DIARY APRIL VOLUME (25) 1917

INTELLIGENCE SUMMARY

(Erase heading not required.)

Place	Date	Hour	Summary of Events and Information	Remarks and references to Appendices
IN THE FIELD	APRIL 1		The Battⁿ moved into billets in BEAVAL	Rfm
	2		The Battⁿ rested in billets in BEAVAL	Rfm
	3		The Battⁿ moved into billets in BOUQUEMAISON	Rfm
	4		The Battⁿ moved into billets in CROISETTE	Rfm
	5		" " rested "	Rfm
	6		" " " "	Rfm
	7		The Battⁿ moved into billets in BUNEVILLE	Rfm
	8		" " " " AMBRINES	Rfm
	9		The Battⁿ moved into billets in HAUTEVILLE	Rfm
	10		" " " " ARRAS	Rfm
	11		The Battⁿ commenced work on the TILLOY-WANCOURT RD	Rfm
	12		The Battⁿ carried out work on TILLOY-WANCOURT } roads TILLOY-BEAURAINS }	Rfm
	13		do do	Rfm
	14		do do	Rfm
	15		do do TILLOY-WANCOURT RD	Rfm
	16		do do	Rfm
	17		do do	Rfm
	18		do do	Rfm
	19		Two companies worked on TILLOY-WANCOURT RD	Rfm

7th DURHAM LIGHT INFANTRY (PIONEERS)   WAR DIARY or INTELLIGENCE SUMMARY   APRIL   VOLUME (25)   Army Form C. 2118.

Place	Date	Hour	Summary of Events and Information	Remarks and references to Appendices
IN THE FIELD	APRIL 20		The Batt'n worked on the TILLOY-WANCOURT.RD.	Rpm
	21		do do	Rpm
	22		One Coy worked on the TILLOY-WANCOURT.RD. Two Coys worked on Strong point in reserve line, one Coy in front of reserve line shelling and drains.	Rpm
	23		One Coy worked on road in WANCOURT village. Two Coys worked in WANCOURT VILLAGE.	Rpm
	24		Two Coys worked on strong point, one Coy infants shelters & carried out wiring in front of reserve line	Rpm
	25		One Bn worked on roads in WANCOURT VILLAGE. Three Coys carried out wiring in front of support line	Rpm
	26		The Batt'n rested in billets in ARRAS	Rpm Rpm
	27		The batt'n moved into billets in COULLEMONT.	Rpm
	28			Rpm
	29		The Batt'n rested in billets at COULLEMONT	Rpm
	30		" " " "	Rpm

7th Durham L. I. Pioneers   1-4-19.

OPERATION ORDERS No. 7.

1. The Battalion will move to BEAUVAL to-morrow, and will parade at 9-50. A.M. in OXFORD STREET in the following order:- Signallers, Div. Band, "A", "B", "C", "D" Coys., Lewis Gun Detachment, "A" Echelon Transport, "B" Echelon Transport, Headquarters Details, with the head of the column at the Cross Roads N.E. of S. of TALMAS [LENS.II.]

2. Blankets in bundles of 10 will be collected by Coys and stacked in four dumps & ready for collection by G.S. Wagons at 7-30.A.M. Details will arrange for their blankets to be placed on one of the Company dumps. All Coys will send one man to the Transport Officer at 7-15.A.M to guide the wagons to the respective dumps. These blankets will be conveyed to the Cross Roads where they will be placed on a motor lorry. 1 Officer and 6 men from "B" will act as a loading party and will be at the Cross Roads to meet the lorry at 7-0.A.M. Coys will arrange for parties to load the G.S. Wagons.

3. Officer's valises and mess kit will be placed on the same dumps by 8-30. A.M.

4. Maltese cart, Cookers & Dixies will be collected at 8-30. A.M.

(Sgd). W. F. Laing
Capt. & Adjutant

7th Bn. D.L.I. Pioneers. Operation Orders No 9.

1. The Battalion will move to CROISETTE and WIGNACOURT area to-morrow. "A" Coy, "D" Coy, Lewis Gun Detachment and Transport will parade in RUE ST LEGER at 8-30.A.M. with the head of the column at the Cross Roads West of the Church facing West.
This party will then proceed up RUE ST POL and will be joined by the remainder of the Battalion which will then be in the following order,- Signallers, "A" Coy "D" Coy, Drum & Bugle Band, "B" Coy, "C" Coy, Lewis Gun Det, L.O. Details, "A" Echelon, "B" Echelon Transport.
2. Blankets in bundles of 10 will be taken to the Q.M. Stores by 7-0.A.M.
3. Officers Valises & Mess kit will be ready for collection by 7-30.A.M..
4. Div. time will be sent round at 7- A.M.

(Sgd) W. F. Laing.
Capt. & Adjutant

3-4-18.

7th Bn. D.L.I. (Pioneers)   SECRET

Operation Orders No. 10.   6-4-17.

1. The Battalion will move to BUNEVILLE to-morrow and will parade at 10. A.M. as under:—

"A" Coy, "B" Coy, Band, L.G. Det, H.Q. Details, on the St. Pol Road with head of the column facing S.E. at road junction beside the Church.

"C" Coy, "D" Coy, & Transport in RUE D'OEUF with head of column facing N.W. at Road junction beside the Church.

2. Blankets (in bundles of 10) from "A" Coy, "B" Coy, Band, Lewis Gun Det, H.Q. Details will be dumped outside Q.M. Stores at 8-30. A.M.

The Q.M. will arrange for the lorry to collect Blankets belonging to "C" Coy, "D" Coy, and Transport at 8-0. A.M.

3. Officers Valises and Mess kit will be ready for collection at 8-30. A.M.

4. Maltese cart, cookers, and dixies will be collected at 8-30. A.M.

5. Water Bottles will be filled.

6. 500 yards will be maintained between the Battalion and 1st line Transport.

7. 1 N.C.O. and 6 men (unfit for marching) will report to Q.M. Stores at 8-30 A.M. in full marching order for loading lorry.

(Sgd) W. F. Laing.
Capt. & Adjutant

P.T.O

Battalion Orders by Lieut: Col, E. Vaux C.M.G., D.S.O., V.D.,
Commanding Pioneer Bn.   6/3/17.

1. REVEILLE :- 7 a.m.
   BREAKFAST :- 7.30 a.m.

2. BILLETING PARTY :-   Captain R.G. Macintyre, 2/Lieut.
   E.R. Manley, 10 Lewis Gunners, and 2 Cyclists, will leave
   the road junction beside the Church at 7 a.m.

3. SLOW PARTY :-   The Slow Party will parade
   under 2/Lieut. J.C. Scott at the Road Junction
   at 10 a.m.

                                    Sgd. W.O. Laing
                                    Capt. & Adjutant.

P.T.O

7th Bn Durham Light Infantry (Pioneers) SECRET
OPERATION ORDERS. No. 11.   7-4-17

1. The Battalion will move to AMBRINES to-morrow via MONTS-EN-TERNOIS-GOUY. and will parade in the main street at 9-50.A.M. with the head of the column facing E. opposite billet occupied by Band in the following order:—
"B" Coy., "A" Coy., Band., "D" Coy., "C" Coy., Lewis Gun Detachment, Headquarters Details, Transport.

2. BLANKETS:-
Blankets (in bundles of 10) will be dumped outside of Q.M. Stores at 8-30.A.M.

3. Officers Valises and Mess kit will be ready for collection at 9-0.A.M.

4. Maltese cart, cookers, and dixies will be collected at 9-0.A.M.

5. Water Bottles will be filled.

6. 500 yards will be maintained between the Battalion and 1st line Transport.

7. 1 N.C.O and 6 men from "C" Coy (unfit for marching) will report to Q.M. Stores at 8-30 A.M. in full marching order for loading lorry.

(Sgd) W. F. Laing.
Capt. & Adjutant

7th Bn Durham L.I Pioneers   SECRET

OPERATION ORDERS No. 12.   9-10-17.

1. The Battalion will march to ARRAS to-morrow morning and will parade at 10-0.am. as under:-
"C" Coy, Bugle Band, "B" Coy, "A" Coy, Lewis Gun Detachment, Div. Band, H.Q. Details, Transport in RUE-de-MOULIN with head of the column at the road junction beside "C" Coy's Officers Mess.
Signallers & "D" Coy will parade on Main Road with head of column at the above road junction.

2. Officers Valises, Mess kit, Maltese cart, Cookers, Dixies etc, will be collected at 9.A.M.

3. Blankets will be carried on the packs. Every endeavour should be made to have blankets rolled uniformly.

4. Haversack rations will be carried.

5. Battalion time will be sent round at 8.30.am

6. N.C.O's and men certified unfit for marching will parade at road junction at 10.am under Lieut. W.L. Campbell.

(Sgd). W.F. Laing.
Capt & Adjutant

7th D.L.I. (Pioneers)

SECRET

OPERATION ORDER No 13.

1. The Battalion less "C" Coy will move by tactical train to-morrow to WARLUZEL.

2. The Battalion will form up between passenger station and goods station at G.28.c.4.3 in the following order:—
"A", "B", "D" Coys, Lewis Gun Detachment.

The Div: Band, Bugle Band, Signallers and all details will parade with the Lewis Gun Detachment.

The time of entrainment will be notified later.

3. The transport, less transport of "C" Coy will move via main ARRAS–DOULLENS road, with the 151st Brigade transport.

Time of departure will be notified later.

4. Drums of the Bugle Band will be carried on the valise wagon.

The Signalling Sergt. will arrange with the Quartermaster to have all signalling gear taken on the cooks wagon.

O.C. Coys and O.C. Details will enforce the strictest discipline during entraining and detraining. No shouting or jumping in and out of carriages is to take place.

All billets must be left clean.

O.C. Coys and details will render a report to the Adjutant, to the effect that billets have been left clean.

(Sgd) R.G. Macintyre.
Capt. & Adjutant

SECRET

ADDENDUM No 1 to Operation Order No. 13.

1. Paras 1 and 2 of Operation Order No. 13 are cancelled.
The Bn. will move by tactical train to COULLEMONT.

2. The Bn. will parade with the head of the column opposite No. 31 Rue EMILE LENGLET at 4 p.m. in the following order :-
    A B D Coys, Lewis Gun Detachment & all details.
Blankets will be carried on the man.

3. The Transport Officer will receive orders from the Brigade T.O., 151 Bgde., as to time of starting. Starting point - Road Junction just south of the I of ARRAS CITADELLE (L.35.b.5.8.). Route to starting point via ACHICOURT.
Head of column to pass starting point at 2.30 p.m.

4. All Officers' Valises and Coy. Mess gear will be outside billets at 12.45 p.m. ready for removal.
The Maltese Cart will be loaded ready to move off at 1 p.m.
Hdqrs. Mess Cart will be at Hdqrs. Mess at 12.45 p.m.
Cookers will be ready for removal at 1 p.m.
All dixies will be at 2.M. Stores at 12.45 p.m.
One baggage wagon before loading up with valises will call at Orderly Room for Orderly Room gear.
O.C. 'C' Coy. will detail one Coy. G.S. Wagon to go round billets after they are vacated to collect all refuse.

Sgd. R.G. Macintyre
Captain & Adjutant

27/4/17.

7th Bn. D.L.I. (Pioneers)

SECRET
30-4-17

OPERATION ORDERS. No 14.

1. The Battalion will march to-morrow May 1st, to POMMIER.

2. The Battalion will parade in full marching order with the head of the column opposite Orderly Room at 2 P.M. in the following order:—

   Signallers, "A" Coy, "B" Coy, "D" Coy, Lewis Gun Detachment, Details, and Transport, steel helmets will be worn.

   There will be an interval of 500 yards between the rear of the Battalion and the Transport.

3. Blankets will be rolled in bundles of 10, distinctly labelled and dumped in the following places by 11. A.M:—

   "D" Coy and all Details at Q.M. Stores.
   "A" & "B" Coys, under the archway of their billet.

4. Officers valises and Mess gear will be collected at 1. P.M.
   Cookers will be ready for removal at 1. P.M.
   Maltese cart will be loaded ready for removal by 2 P.M.
   H.Q. limber will be at H.Q. Mess at 1. P.M.
   Orderly Room gear will be ready for removal at 1. P.M.
   Signalling gear will be taken to Q.M. Stores by 12-30.

5. The instruments and stores of the Div: Band and the drums of the Bugle Band will be stored at the 151st Brigade dump. These stores will be ready for removal at 9-30. A.M. One N.C.O. and one man will remain behind at the Stores to take charge of the instruments and gear. They will be rationed by the Town Major.

   Billets must be left clean. A certificate to that effect will be rendered to Orderly Room.

   Strict attention must be paid to march discipline.

   (Signed) R.G. Macintyre
   Capt. & Adjutant

Original.

SECRET.

WAR DIARY

OF

7th Battalion Durham Light Infantry (Pioneers).

Volume XXVI.

May, 1917.

7TH DURHAM LIGHT INFANTRY PIONEERS

WAR DIARY or INTELLIGENCE SUMMARY

MAY 1917. VOLUME 26.

Army Form C. 2118.

Place	Date	Hour	Summary of Events and Information	Remarks and references to Appendices
IN THE FIELD	MAY 1st		The Battalion marched to BOMMIER, and was billeted in this village for one night.	RMcI
	2nd		The Battalion marched to BLAIRVILLE and were billeted in the cellars of this village.	RMcI
	3rd		The Battalion rested in BLAIRVILLE.	RMcI
	4th		The Battalion marched to COULLEMONT, and were billeted in Farms thereat.	RMcI
	5th		The Battalion rested in COULLEMONT	RMcI
	6		do	RMcI
	7		The Batn commenced training in COULLEMONT area.	RMcI
	8		The Batn continued training	RMcI
	9		as above	RMcI
	10		as above	RMcI
	11		as above	RMcI
	12		as above	RMcI
	13		as above	RMcI
	14		as above	RMcI
	15		as above	RMcI

R McIntyre
Captain and Adjutant,
7th Bn. Durham Light Infantry (Pioneers)

7th DURHAM LIGHT INFANTRY PIONEERS

WAR DIARY or INTELLIGENCE SUMMARY

MAY 1917. VOLUME 26.

Army Form C. 2118.

Place	Date	Hour	Summary of Events and Information	Remarks and references to Appendices
IN THE FIELD	MAY 16		The Battalion continued training	Rhm
	17		as above	Rhm
	18		as above	Rhm
	19		as above	Rhm
	20		as above	Rhm
	21		as above	Rhm
	22		as above	Rhm
	23		as above	Rhm
	24		as above. The Battalion moved to COUIN and occupied huts in that area.	Rhm
	25		The Battalion rested.	Rhm
	26		The Battalion carried out training. Special attention being paid to digging by night	Rhm
	27		One Company moved to BAYENCOURT (150 Pole area).	
	28		One company commenced work on the road to BAYENCOURT and East of BAYENCOURT. Two Companies commenced work on the COUIN - COIGNEUX Road and on road in COIGNEUX. One Company was inoculated and rested.	Rhm

Rhmartine
Captain and Adjutant,
7th Bn. Durham Light Infantry (Pioneers).

7TH DURHAM LIGHT INFANTRY (PIONEERS) WAR DIARY or INTELLIGENCE SUMMARY

MAY 1917 VOLUME 26

Army Form C. 2118.

(Erase heading not required.)

Place	Date	Hour	Summary of Events and Information	Remarks and references to Appendices
IN THE FIELD	MAY 28		Work carried on, on roads in BAYENCOURT Village and End of Ft	
	29		Work carried on on the COUIN-COIGNEUX Road. Received orders to be prepared to move the following day and	
	30		One company return to COUIN from BAYENCOURT. The Battalion moved to FONQUEVILLERS and received relief	
	31		Two companies and Headquarters moved to BOYELLES. Two companies moved to BEAURAINS	

P.L. McIntyre
Captain and Adjutant,
7th Bn. Durham Light Infantry (Pioneers).

SECRET

4" D.L.I. (Pioneers)

OPERATION ORDERS No 15.

The Battalion will move to-morrow to the FICHEUX - BLAIREVILLE - RANSART area.

Time of departure will be notified later.

(Sgd) W. G. Macintyre
Capt. & Adjutant

1/5/17

30/4/17

Operation Order No 14

The Battn will march to POMMIER to-morrow May 1st.

The Battn will parade in full marching order with the head of the column opposite Orderly Room at 2 pm in the following order:-

Sgs, 'A' 'B' & 'D' Coys, Lewis Gun Detachment, Details and Transport.

Steel helmets will be worn

There will be an interval of 500 yds between the rear of the Bn & the Transport

Billets must be left clean, a certificate to that effect will be rendered to Orderly Room.

Strict attention must be paid to march discipline.

Sgd R.G. Macintyre
Capt. & Adjutant

7th Bn Durham L.I. (Pioneers)
OPERATION ORDERS No 16.

1. The Battalion will move to-day to CAULLEMONT.
   The Battalion will parade on the main Road at 4-45 pm with the head of the column facing REVEIRE STATION.

(Sgd) R. G. Macintyre
Capt. & Adjutant

5/5/17

7th D.L.I. (Pioneers).

SECRET

ADD. TO OPERATION ORDERS No. 18.

1. The Battalion will parade at 5.20 p.m. today, with the head of the column 100 yds N.E. of billet No. 100 on the POMMIER - BERLES Road, in the following order :- D., B., A Coys, Lewis Gun detachment, Details, and Transport.

On the march there will be an interval of 500 yds, between the transport and the rear of the battalion.

Blankets will be rolled in bundles of ten, distinctly labelled, and taken to transport lines by 3 p.m.

Valises and mess gear will be outside billets, ready for removal at 4.15 p.m.

Maltese cart will be loaded and cookers ready for removal at 4.15 p.m.

Headquarters limber will be ready for removal at 4.15 p.m.

Billets will be left clean, the usual certificate will be rendered.

Signed. R.G. Macintyre
Capt. & Adjutant.

2/5/17

7th Bn. Durham L.I. Pioneers.   SECRET.

MOVEMENT ORDERS No 17.

1. The Battalion will move to COUIN to-morrow, Route,- HUMBERCOURT-MONDICOURT-PAS.

2. The Battalion will parade in full marching order in the main street of CUILLEMONT at X-MN. 1-50.p.m. with the head of the column fifty yards S.W. of Headquarters Mess in the following order:-
"A", "B" Coys, Bugle Band, Divisional Band, "C" & "D" Coys, Lewis Gun Detachment, Transport.

3. Officers valises and mess gear will be outside of billets ready for collection at 1.p.m.
Cook engines and maltese cart will be ready for removal at 1-15.p.m.
One Cook only will proceed with each cooker.

4. All Details will march with their companies.

5. An interval of 50 yards will be maintained between Transport and rear of Battalion

6. The strictest march discipline must be enforced.

7. All billets will be left clean. A certificate will be rendered to the Orderly Room certifying that billets have been left clean.

8. The slow party will march in charge of 2nd Lieut. T.C.SCOTT. Time of departure will be notified later.

V
24:5:17.

(Sgd) R. G. Macintyre.
Capt. & Adjutant.

7th D.L.I. — Pioneers
29.5.17

Operation Orders No 18.

The Battalion will move to FONQUEVILLERS. to-morrow, — Route - COUIN - SOUASTRE — FONQUEVILLERS.

The Battalion will form up at 1.50 p.m. on the road alongside the huts with the head of the column 50 yards past the entrance to the hut camp facing East in the following order:—

Signallers, 'A' and 'B' Coys, Bugle Band, 'C' and 'D' Coys, Lewis Gun Detachment, Burial Party. Details will march with their companies.

Officers valises, Mess gear, Cookers and Maltese cart will be ready for removal at 12.45 p.m.

All Billets will be left clean, a certificate to this effect will be handed into the Orderly Room.

The Transport will form up, at an interval of 50 yards in the rear of the Battalion

Sgd. R. G. Macintyre
Capt. & Adjutant

7th Bn Durham L.I. (Pioneers)

OPERATION ORDERS. No. 19.

1. The Battalion will move to new area to-morrow.

"A" and "B" Companies to BAEURAINS.
The remainder of the Battalion to BOYELLES.

Route :— HANNESCAMPS — BEINVILLERS AU BOIS — MONCHY AU BOIS — ADINFER — BOIRY Ste RICTRUDE.

The Battalion will form up in the main street with the head of the column opposite the Orderly Room at 7-50 A.M. in the following order:—

Signallers, "A" and "B" Coy's, Bugle Band, "C" and "D" Coys, Lewis Gun Detachment, Burial Party. Transport will form up in rear of the Battalion at an interval of 50 yards.

Cookers, Officer's Valises, & Mess gear, will be ready for removal at 7. A.M.

(Sgd) R. G. Macintyre
Capt. & Adjutant

30/5/17.

Original.

SECRET.

WAR DIARY

OF

7th Battalion, The Durham Light Infantry, (Pioneers).

Volume XXVII.

June, 1917.

Army Form C. 2118.

7th DURHAM LIGHT INFANTRY (PIONEERS) WAR DIARY or INTELLIGENCE SUMMARY

JUNE 1917 VOLUME 27.

(Erase heading not required.)

Place	Date	Hour	Summary of Events and Information	Remarks and references to Appendices
In the Field	June 1		Work carried out on the following roads:-	Apps.
			A Coy. NEUVILLE VITASSE — WANCOURT ROAD.	
			B Coy. BEAURAINS — NEUVILLE VITASSE ROAD.	
			NEUVILLE VITASSE — HENIN Road	
			NEUVILLE VITASSE — MERCATEL Road.	
			C Coy. ARRAS — BAPAUME MAIN ROAD — HENIN Road	
			HENIN — ST LEGER Road	
			D Coy. MAISON ROUGE FARM — JUDAS FARM	
			ST LEGER Road.	
			RAILWAY BRIDGE (T.19.a.4.2) — JUDAS COPSE	

Army Form C. 2118.

4th DURHAM LIGHT INFANTRY (PIONEERS) WAR DIARY or INTELLIGENCE SUMMARY

JUNE 1917
VOLUME 24

(Erase heading not required.)

Instructions regarding War Diaries and Intelligence Summaries are contained in F. S. Regs., Part II. and the Staff Manual respectively. Title Pages will be prepared in manuscript.

Place	Date	Hour	Summary of Events and Information	Remarks and references to Appendices
In the Field	June 2		Work continued as above.	App
"	3		do "	App
	4		do	App
	5		do	App
	6		do	App
	7		do	App
	8		do	App
	9		do	App
	10		do	App
	11		do	App

WAR DIARY or INTELLIGENCE SUMMARY

7th DURHAM LIGHT INFANTRY (PIONEERS)

JUNE 1914 VOLUME 24

Army Form C. 2118.

(Erase heading not required.)

Instructions regarding War Diaries and Intelligence Summaries are contained in F. S. Regs., Part II. and the Staff Manual respectively. Title Pages will be prepared in manuscript.

Place	Date	Hour	Summary of Events and Information	Remarks and references to Appendices
In the Field	June 12		Work continued as above	App
	13		do	App
	14		do	App
	15		The following letter received from VII Corps. "To VII th Corps." I should be glad if the good work done by the 7th Durham L.I. (Pioneers) could be brought to the notice of the G.O.C. 50th Division. During the time this Battalion has been employed under me as pioneers Lt Colonel VAUX has shewn exceptional interest in its work with the result that the Battalion has done exceedingly well and excellent work on the roads under their charge which will be of permanent value during next winter. Sgd J.A. Tennant Brigadier General Chief Engineer VII Corps	App

WAR DIARY

7th DURHAM LIGHT INFANTRY (PIONEERS)

INTELLIGENCE SUMMARY

JUNE 1917
VOLUME 24

Army Form C. 2118.

Place	Date	Hour	Summary of Events and Information	Remarks and references to Appendices
In the Field	June 15		Work continued on roads	App.
	16		do	App.
	17		—	
			The Battalion moved to HENIN SHELTERS at T.3.a.4.2. and relieved the 8th SUSSEX (PIONEERS 18th Division).	App.
	18		Work was commenced on the following trenches. Bay on {EARLS COURT / CROW TRENCH} A Coy on FOSTER AVENUE C Coy on SHAWK TRENCH 'D' Coy on AVENUE TRENCH	App.

WAR DIARY or INTELLIGENCE SUMMARY

Army Form C. 2118.

1/7 DURHAM LIGHT INFANTRY (PIONEERS)

JUNE 1917 VOLUME 24

Place	Date	Hour	Summary of Events and Information	Remarks and references to Appendices
In the Field	June 19		Work continued on the before mentioned trenches	Appx
	20		do	Appx
	21		do	Appx
	22		do	Appx
	23		do	Appx
	24		Work commenced by two companies on the following trenches. PUG LANE. WOOD TRENCH.	Appx
	25		Work continued on SHAWK TRENCH and AVENUE TRENCH. Repairs to roads carried out on HENIN-HENINEL R.D.	Appx

R W McIntyre
Captain and Adjutant,
7th Bn. Durham Light Infantry (Pioneers).

Army Form C. 2118.

14th DURHAM LIGHT INFANTRY (PIONEERS) WAR DIARY JUNE 1917
INTELLIGENCE SUMMARY VOLUME 27

(Erase heading not required.)

Instructions regarding War Diaries and Intelligence Summaries are contained in F. S. Regs., Part II. and the Staff Manual respectively. Title Pages will be prepared in manuscript.

Place	Date	Hour	Summary of Events and Information	Remarks and references to Appendices
In the field.	26		Work continued on the following trenches WOOD TRENCH. PUG LANE SHAWK TRENCH AVENUE TRENCH	P.m.
	27		Work continued on HENIN-HENINEL RD	
	28		Work continued as above	P.m.
	29		" " "	P.m.
	30		" " "	P.m.
				P.m.

P. Macintyre
Captain and Adjutant,
14th Bn. Durham Light Infantry (Pioneers),

SECRET

Operation Orders No. 20.   16th June 1917

The Battalion less 'A' Coy, Transport and Q.M. Stores, will move to Shelters at T.3.a.4.2 to-morrow 17th inst.

'A' Coy. will move to huts at T.13.a.5.8.

'B' Coy. will parade at 3 p.m., 'C' Coy. will parade at 3.30 p.m., 'D' Coy. will parade at 4 p.m., 'A' Coy. will parade at 5 p.m.

Details will parade with their companies.

The Transport Officer will arrange to convey what tools are required by 'C' & 'D' Coys (ie. picks & shovels) to T.3.a.4.2. at 10 A.M. to-morrow.

Upon the return of the wagons, the Transport Officer will arrange with O.C. 'C' and 'D' Coys. for conveyance of Officers Valises and Mess Gear.

All Cook Engines will remain at T.13.a.5.8 and dixies only will be taken to T.3.a.4.2.

Headquarters limber and Maltese Cart will be ready for removal at 5 p.m.

'B' Coy. will only take what tools are required to T.3.a.4.2 namely picks and shovels, the remainder of their tools will be conveyed by the other tool wagon to T.13.a.5.8.

'B' Coy. Officers Valises and Mess Gear will be conveyed to T.3.a.4.2 by Limber provided by Transport Officer.

'A' Coy. Officers Valises and Mess Gear will be conveyed to T.13.a.5.8 by the Limber provided by Transport Officer.

O.C. Coys. will render a certificate to Orderly Room that all huts and ground occupied by Companies has been left clean.

Sgd. A. V. Dickinson
2/Lieut & Adjutant.

"War Diary"

Original.

SECRET.

WAR DIARY

OF

7th Battalion, The Durham Light Infantry (Pioneers).

Volume XXVIII.

July, 1917.

7th DURHAM LIGHT INFANTRY (PIONEERS) WAR DIARY
JULY 1917
INTELLIGENCE SUMMARY VOLUME 2 8
Army Form C. 2118.

Place	Date	Hour	Summary of Events and Information	Remarks and references to Appendices
In the field	July 1		Two bays continued work on SHAWK STREET. Two bays " " shelters on the NEUVILLE-VITASSE — WANCOURT RD. Work continued on the HENIN-HENINEL RD.	Rm
	2.		Work continued on SHAWK STREET. Work continued on shelters on the NEUVILLE-VITASSE — WANCOURT RD. 50 men commenced work under orders from the C.E. VII Corps, on the following roads :— HENIN — ST. LEGER. RD. HENIN — CROISILLES. RD. BOIRY-BECQUERELLE — HENIN. RD.	Rm

7th DURHAM LIGHT INFANTRY (PIONEERS)

JULY 1917 Army Form C. 2118.

VOLUME 28.

WAR DIARY or INTELLIGENCE SUMMARY

(Erase heading not required.)

Instructions regarding War Diaries and Intelligence Summaries are contained in F. S. Regs., Part II. and the Staff Manual respectively. Title Pages will be prepared in manuscript.

Place	Date	Hour	Summary of Events and Information	Remarks and references to Appendices
In the Field	July 3		Work continued on SHAWK STREET Shelters on NEUVILLE-VITASSE – WANCOURT RD. under orders of the VII Corps.	Pm
	4		Work continued on SHAWK STREET Shelters. " " under orders of the VII Corps.	Pm
	5		Work continued on SHAWK STREET. " " on SOUTHERN E.T. " " under orders of the VII Corps. Shelters on NEUVILLE-VITASSE – WANCOURT RD. Work commenced on MARLIÈRE – QUEMAPPE cross country track.	Pm

Army Form C. 2118.

7th DURHAM LIGHT INFANTRY (PIONEERS)

JULY 1917 VOLUME 28

WAR DIARY or INTELLIGENCE SUMMARY

(Erase heading not required.)

Instructions regarding War Diaries and Intelligence Summaries are contained in F. S. Regs., Part II. and the Staff Manual respectively. Title Pages will be prepared in manuscript.

Place	Date	Hour	Summary of Events and Information	Remarks and references to Appendices
In the Field	JULY 6		Work continued on SHAWK. STREET.	Reph
			" " SOUTHERN TRENCH. C.T.	
			" " MARLIERE - GUEMAPPE. R.D.	
			Roads under orders of C.E. VII Corps	
	7		ditto	Rem
	8		Work commenced on the 50th Div Ordnance Stores.	Rem
	9		ditto	Rem
	10		ditto	Rem
	11		ditto	Rem

2449 Wt. W14957/M90 750,000 1/16 J.B.C. & A. Forms/C.2118/12.

Army Form C. 2118.

7th DURHAM LIGHT INFANTRY (PIONEERS)
WAR DIARY or INTELLIGENCE SUMMARY
JULY 1917 VOLUME N° 8

(Erase heading not required.)

Instructions regarding War Diaries and Intelligence Summaries are contained in F.S. Regs., Part II. and the Staff Manual respectively. Title Pages will be prepared in manuscript.

Place	Date	Hour	Summary of Events and Information	Remarks and references to Appendices
In the Field	July, 12		Work continued on the following trenches:- SOUTHERN C.T. SHAWK ST. C.T.	Pnrs.
	13		Work commenced on FOSTER AVENUE. Work continued CUENAPPE RD.	Pnrs.
	14		C.E. VIII LE & infra. Ditto. Ditto.	Pnrs.
	15		Ditto. Work commenced on KESTRAL AVENUE. ditto	Pnrs.
	16		Work commenced on SHIKAR. ditto	Pnrs.

Army Form C. 2118.

7. BATT. DURHAM. LIGHT. INFANTRY. (PIONEERS) WAR DIARY JULY 1917.
INTELLIGENCE SUMMARY VOLUME 28

Instructions regarding War Diaries and Intelligence Summaries are contained in F. S. Regs., Part II. and the Staff Manual respectively. Title Pages will be prepared in manuscript.

(Erase heading not required.)

Place	Date	Hour	Summary of Events and Information	Remarks and references to Appendices
In the field	JULY 16		A and D. Coys. dug a new front line long January up DEAD BOSCHE SAP to BYKER. SAP. Work continued on SHIKAR AVENUE FOSTER.	Bonn
			Roads widened & others of VII It & others widened	
	17		Work continued on new front line. Trench widened and deepened. Work continued on SHIKAR AVENUE FOSTER.	Bonn
			Roads widened & orders of VII It & others between C.T. between SWIFT and	
	18		A and D. Coys. dug new C.T. between CURTAIN. TR. Work continued on SHIKAR AVENUE FOSTER.	Bonn
			Roads widened orders of VII to others	

2449 Wt. W14957/M90 750,000 1/16 J.B.C. & A. Forms/C.2118/12.

Army Form C. 2118.

7th DURHAM LIGHT INFANTRY (PIONEERS) WAR DIARY or INTELLIGENCE SUMMARY

JULY 1917. VOLUME 28.

Instructions regarding War Diaries and Intelligence Summaries are contained in F. S. Regs., Part II. and the Staff Manual respectively. Title Pages will be prepared in manuscript.

(Erase heading not required.)

Place	Date	Hour	Summary of Events and Information	Remarks and references to Appendices
In the field	JULY 19		Work continued on new C.T. between SWIFT & CURTAIN T.R. Work continued on SHIKAR AVENUE. Work continued on new front line trench between BYKER & DEAD BOSCHE SAP. Work continued on roads under orders of VII th Corps	Reen.
	20		Work carried out on KESTRAL C.T. " " " FOSTER AVENUE. 450 yards of new C.T. dug from CURTAIN T.R. towards CUCKOO TRENCH. Work continued on Roads under VII th Corps orders. Work continued on KESTRAL C.T.S. SOUTHERN. FOSTER.	Reen.
	21		A new trench was dug by parties in BYKERS.AP & OTTO SAP. Work continued on roads under VII th Corps orders.	Reen.

7th Battn. DURHAM LIGHT INFANTRY (PIONEERS)   WAR DIARY or INTELLIGENCE SUMMARY   JULY 1917   VOLUME 28   Army Form C. 2118.

Place	Date	Hour	Summary of Events and Information	Remarks and references to Appendices
In the field.	JULY 22.		Work continued on new trench between BYKER & OTTO SAPS KESTRAL AVENUE SOUTHERN " SHIKAR " Work continued on road under VII Corps orders.	Pen.
	23.		New support trench dug between WREN TRENCH to new point of new C.T. between SWIFT & CUCKOO. Work continued on new C.T. between SWIFT & CUCKOO	Pen.
	24		Work continued on new support between WREN TR. 15 new point to new C.T. Work continued on new C.T. between SWIFT & CUCKOO under orders of VII Corps.	Pen.

7th DURHAM LIGHT INFANTRY   **WAR DIARY**   VOLUME 28.
(PIONEERS)   or   **INTELLIGENCE SUMMARY**   JULY 1917

Army Form C. 2118.

Instructions regarding War Diaries and Intelligence Summaries are contained in F.S. Regs., Part II. and the Staff Manual respectively. Title Pages will be prepared in manuscript.

(Erase heading not required.)

Place	Date	Hour	Summary of Events and Information	Remarks and references to Appendices
In the Field				
	24.		Work continued on roads under VII Corps.	
	25.		Work continued on new C.T. PIONEER ALLEY.	
			Work commenced of FOSTER AVENUE.	Plan
			do continued of SOUTHERN AVENUE.	
			do do SHIKAR	
			do do KESTRAL AVENUE	
	26.		Work continued on PIONEER ALLEY.	
			" " FOSTER AVENUE	
			" " KESTRAL "	
			" " Roads under VII Corps.	Plan
	27.		Work continued of KESTRAL, AVENUE	
			" " FOSTER AVENUE	
			New support trench dug between PIONEER ALLEY and LARK LANE.	Plan

7th DURHAM LIGHT INFANTRY (PIONEERS)

VOLUME 28.
JULY 1917

WAR DIARY
or
INTELLIGENCE SUMMARY
(Erase heading not required.)

Army Form C. 2118.

Place	Date	Hour	Summary of Events and Information	Remarks and references to Appendices
In the field	July 28.		Work continued on FOSTER AVENUE.	D.m.
			" " " KESTRAL AVENUE.	
			" " new support trench from PIONEER ALLEY to	
			LARK LANE.	
	29.		Work continued on main trench VII.4 to own orders	D.m.
			Work continued on PIONEER ALLEY.	
			FOSTER AVENUE.	
			KESTRAL AVENUE.	
			Roads under VII.4 to own orders	
	30		ditto	D.m.
	31		ditto	D.m.

Captain and Adjutant,
7th Bn. Durham Light Infantry (Pioneers).

SECRET.

WAR DIARY

of

7th. BN. DURHAM LIGHT INFANTRY

(PIONEERS).

Volume XXIX.

August 1917.

7th DURHAM LIGHT INFANTRY (PIONEERS)

WAR DIARY or INTELLIGENCE SUMMARY

Army Form C. 2118.

VOLUME 29.
AUGUST 1917.

Place	Date	Hour	Summary of Events and Information	Remarks and references to Appendices
In the field	August 1		Work continued on the following trenches:- PIONEER ALLEY, FOSTER AVENUE, KESTRAL ", SHIKAR ", SOUTHERN ", new support line running from WREN to LARK LANE through PIONEER ALLEY. ROADS under 7 th labour orders.	Pam
	2		Work continued as on previous day.	Pam
			Work continued on CUCKOO TRENCH	
	3		Work continues as on previous day.	Pam
	4		ditto	Pam
	5		ditto	Pam
			KESTRAL AVENUE joined up with BISON TRENCH	

7th DURHAM LIGHT INFANTRY (PIONEERS)

WAR DIARY or INTELLIGENCE SUMMARY

Army Form C. 2118.

VOLUME 29 AUGUST 1917.

Place	Date	Hour	Summary of Events and Information	Remarks and references to Appendices
In the field	6		Work continued on the following trenches :— FOSTER AVENUE. KESTRAL do PIONEER ALLEY. CUCKOO SUPPORT. SOUTHERN AVENUE SHAWK STREET. NEW TRENCH between KESTRAL AVENUE and BISON TR. ROADS — VII. to own orders.	Pm
	7		ditto	Pm
	8		ditto	Pm
	9		Work continued on FOSTER AVENUE, new front line, a drug between SOUTHERN AV. and DURHAM ALLEY. Work continued on roads under VII. to own orders.	Pm

7th Battn. The DURHAM LIGHT INFANTRY (PIONEERS)   WAR DIARY or INTELLIGENCE SUMMARY   Army Form C. 2118.

VOLUME 29   AUGUST 1917.

Place	Date	Hour	Summary of Events and Information	Remarks and references to Appendices
In the field	August 10		Work continued on FOSTER AVENUE & KESTRAL AVENUE Roads.	Rem.
	11		Work carried out on HOE SUPPORT. Continued on front line trench between SOUTHERN AVENUE & DURHAM ALLEY.	Rem.
	12		Roads work carried out on HENINEL – CHERISY RD. Revetting of FOSTER AVENUE continued. Work continued on HOE TRENCH FRONT LINE between SOUTHERN AVENUE and DURHAM ALLEY. Work continued on cross trenches between ... ROADS	Rem.

7th Batt. DURHAM LIGHT INFANTRY.
(PIONEERS)

Army Form C. 2118.

WAR DIARY
INTELLIGENCE SUMMARY

VOLUME 29
AUGUST 1917

Place	Date	Hour	Summary of Events and Information	Remarks and references to Appendices
In the Field.	August 13		Revetting of FOSTER AVENUE continued. HOE SUPPORT completed. Work continued on roads.	Pm
	14		Revetting continued on FOSTER AVENUE. Work continued on Roads.	Pm
	15		Work commenced on BORDER LANE. Revetting continued in FOSTER AVENUE. Work continued on Roads.	Pm
	16		Revetting continued in FOSTER AVENUE. BORDER LANE completed. Work continued on Roads.	Pm

Army Form C. 2118.

"7th Bn. DURHAM LIGHT INFANTRY
(PIONEERS)"

WAR DIARY
or
INTELLIGENCE SUMMARY

VOLUME 4
AUGUST 1917

(Erase heading not required.)

Instructions regarding War Diaries and Intelligence Summaries are contained in F.S. Regs., Part II. and the Staff Manual respectively. Title Pages will be prepared in manuscript.

Place	Date	Hour	Summary of Events and Information	Remarks and references to Appendices
In the field.	August 17		Work commenced on C.T. leading from front line to APE SUPPORT. Revetting continued on FOSTER AVENUE. Work continued on huts.	
	18		Revetting continued in FOSTER AVENUE. Work continued on huts. Work continued on C.T. between front line & APE SUPPORT.	
	19		Ditto	
			Work commenced on DURHAM ALLEY. FOSTER AVENUE completed.	
	20		Work continued on DURHAM ALLEY. Work commenced on AVENUE TRENCH.	
	21		Work continued on floors.	
	22		Ditto	

2449 Wt. W14957/M90 750,000 1/16 J.B.C. & A. Forms/C.2118/12.

7ᵗʰ DURHAM LIGHT INFANTRY (PIONEERS)

WAR DIARY or INTELLIGENCE SUMMARY

VOLUME 29. AUGUST 1917

Army Form C. 2118.

Place	Date	Hour	Summary of Events and Information	Remarks and references to Appendices
In the field	August 23		Work continued on AVENUE TRENCH.	
	24		Work continued on Roads. Commenced to erect stables at BOIRY BECQUERELLE for Battalion transport.	
	25		ditto	
			Work carried out on support trench running from LARK LANE to SWALLOW LANE. All work greatly hindered by extremely wet weather.	
	26		No work done on account of wet.	
	27		Wet weather continues. No work done.	
	28		Revetment of SHIKAR AVENUE commenced.	
	29		Revetments continued on SHIKAR AV. Work done on LARK LANE. Revetting done to BORDER LANE.	

7th Battn DURHAM LIGHT INFANTRY (PIONEERS) WAR DIARY

Volume 29

INTELLIGENCE SUMMARY

AUGUST 1917

Army Form C. 2118.

Place	Date	Hour	Summary of Events and Information	Remarks and references to Appendices
In the field	August 30		Work continued on BORDERLANE & SHIKAR AV.	Plan
			Revetment of PIONEER ALLEY commenced.	
	31		Work continued on HENINEL-CHERISY RD.	Plan
			ditto	
			ditto	

P. J. McIntyre
Captain and Adjutant,
7th Bn. Durham Light Infantry (Pioneers).

WAR DIARY

of

7TH. BATTN. DURHAM LIGHT INFANTRY.

(PIONEERS).

VOLUME XXX.

SEPTEMBER 1917.

Army Form C. 2118.

7th DURHAM LIGHT INFANTRY (PIONEERS) WAR DIARY Volume 30
or
INTELLIGENCE SUMMARY SEPTEMBER 1917

(Erase heading not required.)

Instructions regarding War Diaries and Intelligence Summaries are contained in F. S. Regs., Part II and the Staff Manual respectively. Title Pages will be prepared in manuscript.

Place	Date	Hour	Summary of Events and Information	Remarks and references to Appendices
IN THE FIELD	SEPT 1		Revetting of SHIKAR AVENUE continued " " PIONEER ALLEY " " " BORDER LANE " Work continued on HENIN EL-CHERISY RD.	Pym
	2		Revetting of SHIKAR AVENUE continued " PIONEER ALLEY " BORDER LANE Work continued on HENINEL CHERISY RD.	Pym
	3		ditto	Pym

2449 Wt. W14957/M90 750,000 1/16 J.B.C. & A. Forms/C.2118/12.

Army Form C. 2118.

7th BATTN. DURHAM LIGHT INFANTRY (PIONEERS)

WAR DIARY or INTELLIGENCE SUMMARY

VOLUME 30.

SEPTEMBER. 1917

(Erase heading not required.)

Instructions regarding War Diaries and Intelligence Summaries are contained in F. S. Regs., Part II. and the Staff Manual respectively. Title Pages will be prepared in manuscript.

Place	Date	Hour	Summary of Events and Information	Remarks and references to Appendices
IN THE FIELD.	SEPT. 4.		Work continued on SHIKAR AVENUE. " " " PIONEER ALLEY. " " " HENINEL-CHERISY. RD.	Plan
	5		New stables for the transport of the batt. completed. Work continued on PIONEER ALLEY. " " " SHIKAR AVENUE. " " " HENINEL & CHERISY RD.	Plan
	6		Work continued to PIONEER ALLEY. " " " SHIKAR AVENUE " " " HENINEL-CHERISY.RD. " " " CUCKOO RESERVE Work commenced on ROAD running into WANCOURT.	Plan

7th Bde DURHAM LIGHT INFANTRY (PIONEERS)

WAR DIARY or INTELLIGENCE SUMMARY

Army Form C. 2118.
VOLUME 30 SEPTEMBER 1917

Place	Date	Hour	Summary of Events and Information	Remarks and references to Appendices
THE FIELD	SEPT 7		Work continued on PIONEER ALLEY. ,, ,, ,, SHIKAR AVENUE ,, ,, ,, CUCKOO RESERVE ,, ,, ,, HENINEL-CHERISY. RD. ,, ,, ,, ROAD running into WANCOURT from TILLOY.	[sig]
	8		Work continued on SHIKAR AVENUE ,, ,, ,, CUCKOO RESERVE ,, ,, ,, PIONEER ALLEY. ,, ,, ,, HENINEL-CHERISY.RD. ,, ,, ,, Road running into WANCOURT from TILLOY	[sig]
	9		Work continued on SHIKAR AVENUE ,, ,, ,, PIONEER ALLEY ,, ,, ,, HENINEL CHERISY. RD. ,, ,, ,, WANCOURT ROAD.	[sig]

7th BATTN. DURHAM LIGHT INFANTRY (PIONEERS)

WAR DIARY or **INTELLIGENCE SUMMARY**

Army Form C. 2118.
VOLUME 20
SEPTEMBER 1917

Place	Date	Hour	Summary of Events and Information	Remarks and references to Appendices
IN THE FIELD	10.		Work continued on SHIKAR AVENUE	Plan
			PIONEER ALLEY	
			CUCKOO RESERVE	
			FOSTER AVENUE	
			HENINEL - CHERISY RD.	
			WANCOURT - RD	
	11		Work commenced on new front line trench running from	
			WREN-LANE to CABLE SAP.	
			Work continued on HENINEL - CHERISY - RD.	Plan.
			WANCOURT ROAD.	
			new trench between WREN LANE and CABLE SAP (completed)	
	12		Work continued on SHIKAR. AV.	Plan
			" " " WANCOURT - NEUVILLE-VITASSE RD	
			" " " HENINEL - CHERISY.	

7th Batt. DURHAM LIGHT INFANTRY (PIONEERS)

WAR DIARY or INTELLIGENCE SUMMARY

VOLUME 30. SEPTEMBER 1917.

Army Form C. 2118.

Place	Date	Hour	Summary of Events and Information	Remarks and references to Appendices
In the Field	13.		Work continued on SHIKAR AV. C.T.	Sd Bar Capt & Adjt
			" " NEUVILLE-VITASSE — WANCOURT. RD.	
			" " HENINEL - CHERISY Road	
	13-14		Front line between BORDER LANE and BYKER JAP (O.25/. and O.26/.) deepened & widened by two Coys [A + B]	
	14		Work continued on NEUVILLE-VITASSE — WANCOURT Road	Sd Bar Capt & Adjt
			" " " HENINEL - CHERISY Road	
			" " " SHIKAR AVENUE C.T.	
	14-15		Portions of F.L. in O.25/. and O.26/. deepened where necessary (2 Platoons)	
	16		WORK CONTINUED ON NEUVILLE-VITASSE - WANCOURT. RD.	RBm
			" " " HENINEL - CHERISY RD.	
			" " " SHIKAR AVENUE C.T.	
			" " " CUCKOO RESERVE TR.	

7th Batt: DURHAM LIGHT INFANTRY (PIONEERS)

Army Form C. 2118.

Volume 30

WAR DIARY
or
INTELLIGENCE SUMMARY

September 1917

Place	Date	Hour	Summary of Events and Information	Remarks and references to Appendices
In the FIELD	17.		Work continued on NEUVILLE-VITASSE-WANCOURT.RD. HENINEL-CHERISY.RD. SHIKAR.AVENUE.CT. CUCKOO RESERVE.TR. FOSTER AVENUE from the QUARRY EASTWARDS	Rem
	18		Work continued on NEUVILLE-VITASSE WANCOURT RD. " " HENINEL-CHERISY RD. " " SHIKAR.AVENUE CT. " " FOSTER AVENUE CT. Work commenced on SOUTHERN.AVENUE.CT. " " SWALLOW.LANE. The Revetting of CUCKOO RESERVE completed Work continued on FOSTER AVENUE.CT.	
	19.		" " SHIKAR.AV. CT. " " SWALLOW LANE.CT. " " SOUTHERN AVENUE.CT. Revetting Memorial Cree.	

7th DURHAM LIGHT INFANTRY. (PIONEERS). WAR DIARY or INTELLIGENCE SUMMARY

Army Form C. 2118.

VOLUME 30.
SEPTEMBER 1917

Place	Date	Hour	Summary of Events and Information	Remarks and references to Appendices
In the FIELD	September 20		Work continued on SHIKAR AVENUE. C.T.	Pom.
			" " " SOUTHERN AVENUE. C.T.	
			" " " FOSTER AV. C.T.	
			" " " SWALLOW LANE	
			" " " Roads in Divisional area.	
	21		ditto	Pom.
	22		ditto	Pom.
	23		Work commenced on the WANCOURT-MARLIÈRE RD.	Pom.
			Work continued on SOUTHERN AV. C.T.	
			" " " SHIKAR AV. C.T.	
			" " " FOSTER AV. C.T.	
			" " " SWALLOW LANE	
			" " " Roads in Divisional area.	

7th Bn. DURHAM LIGHT INFANTRY (PIONEERS)

WAR DIARY or INTELLIGENCE SUMMARY

Army Form C. 2118.

VOLUME 30
SEPTEMBER, 1917.

Place	Date	Hour	Summary of Events and Information	Remarks and references to Appendices
In the FIELD.	SEPT. 24		Work continued on SOUTHERN AV. CT.	Pem
			" " SHIKAR AV.	
			" " FOSTER. AV.	
			" " SWALLOW. LANE.	
			" " WANCOURT-MARLIERE.RD.	
			" " WANCOURT-TILLOY.RD.	
			" " HENINEL-CHERISY.RD.	
	25.		Work continued on SOUTHERN. CT.	Pem
			" " FOSTER. AV.	
			" " SWALLOW. LANE.	
			" " WANCOURT-MARLIERE.RD.	
			" " WANCOURT-TILLOY.RD.	
	26		ditto	Pem
	27		ditto	Pem

7th DURHAM LIGHT INFANTRY (PIONEERS)

WAR DIARY or **INTELLIGENCE SUMMARY**

Army Form C. 2118.
VOLUME 30
SEPTEMBER 1917

Place	Date	Hour	Summary of Events and Information	Remarks and references to Appendices
In the FIELD	28		Work continued on SOUTHERN AVENUE FOSTER " FIRST " HENINEL - CHERISY Road TILLOY - WANCOURT "	
In the Field	29		Work continued on SOUTHERN AVENUE FOSTER " FIRST " HENINEL - CHERISY Road TILLOY - WANCOURT " Wire put out in front of HINDEN BURG LINE	
	30		ditto	Remainder bayu + coy. 7/D25 (Pioneers)

WAR DIARY

of

7TH. BN. DURHAM LIGHT INFANTRY

(PIONEERS).

VOLUME XXXI.

OCTOBER 1917.

7th Batt DURHAM LIGHT INFANTRY (PIONEERS)

VOLUME 31.

OCTOBER 1917

Army Form C. 2118.

WAR DIARY or INTELLIGENCE SUMMARY

Place	Date	Hour	Summary of Events and Information	Remarks and references to Appendices
In the FIELD	October 1.		Work continued on SOUTHERN AVENUE C.T. AVENUE TRENCH C.T. NEUVILLE-VITASSE — WANCOURT RD.	P.9h
	2		Work commenced widening & deepening PANTHER TRENCH. ditto	
			The wiring of HINDENBURGH — SUPPORT continued.	P.9m
	3		One Coy moved to the COURCELLES AREA, to improve ranges etc for training Wiring of the HINDENBURGH LINE continued Work continued on AVENUE TR. PANTHER TR.	P.9m

7th DURHAM LIGHT INFANTRY (PIONEERS)   VOLUME 31   Army Form C. 2118.

WAR DIARY or INTELLIGENCE SUMMARY

OCTOBER 1917

(Erase heading not required.)

Instructions regarding War Diaries and Intelligence Summaries are contained in F. S. Regs., Part II. and the Staff Manual respectively. Title Pages will be prepared in manuscript.

Place	Date	Hour	Summary of Events and Information	Remarks and references to Appendices
In the FIELD	October 3		Wiring continued in front of HINDENBURG LINE. Double D.T.A. Wire entanglement completed from EARL'S COURT to HENINEL. Strong posts on CORD LINE repaired.	J.J.
	4		Work on CORD LINE Strong posts continued.	J.J.
	5		The Battalion left the Corps, moved to CORCELLES-LES-LENS area and were billeted two Coys. in the village and one in huts.	J.J. Vide operation order No. 21.
	6		The Battalion attended the whole Church parade. Commencement of the training.	J.J.
	7		The Battalion commenced training. A beginning was made in Infantry training with squad & drill., Rifle Exercises and P.T. 'B' company rejoined the Battalion.	J.J.
	8		As above. Training was carried on.	J.J.
	9			

Army Form C. 2118.

WAR DIARY
or
INTELLIGENCE SUMMARY

(Erase heading not required.)

LIGHT INFANTRY (PIONEERS)

VOLUME 31.
OCTOBER 1917.

7th Bn DURHAM

Place	Date	Hour	Summary of Events and Information	Remarks and references to Appendices
In the Field	10		As above. A draft of 210 men an equal number to the Ex D.L.I. reinforcements received 22-9-17 were sent to the 5th D.L.I. 70, to the 6th D.L.I. 70, and to the 9th D.L.I. 70.	1
	11		As above. Training programme carried on	1
	12		As above	
	13		As above	
	14		Church parade was training programme	1 C.B
	15		Training programme carried on	1
	16		As above	J.C.B
	17		As above	
	18		The Battalion less one company entrains at BAPAUME and moves to EQUELBECQ. 'B' company entrained at MIRAMONT and moved to CASSEL. The Battalion went into billets in the LA CLOCHE area. (S.H. HAZEBROUCK)	1 A.B Vide O.O. No 22.
	19		In Billets as above	Ref. P.R.
	20		The Battalion marched to PROVEN and were billeted in a tent camp at (Sheet 27. F.7. D.4.6)	Vide O.O. No 23 N.F.F.

2449 Wt. W14957/M90 750,000 1/16 J.B.C. & A. Forms/C.2118/12.

WAR DIARY
or
7th Bn DURHAM INTELLIGENCE SUMMARY
(Erase heading not required.)

LIGHT INFANTRY (PIONEERS)

Army Form C. 2118.

Volume 31

OCTOBER 1917.

Place	Date	Hour	Summary of Events and Information	Remarks and references to Appendices
In the Field	21st to 23rd		In camp as above.	W.P.L.
	24th		The Battalion moved to WHITE MILL CAMP ELVERDINGHE (B.14.d.65. Sheet 28)	note O.O. N⁰ 2
	25th		Work commenced by the four Companies assisted by an Infantry carrying party in completing and repairing RAILWAY STREET (a track Board track running N the North of the Railway from about B.12.B.5.7. to V.I.C.5.4. (Sheet 20) Work as above. The Lewis Gun Detachment are in forward posts to deal with low flying enemy aircraft.	W.P.L.
	26th			W.P.L.
	27th		Work as above. In spite of the severe shelling, mud and long carries the Companies have done splendid work and the Duck Board track is of great assistance to the Infantry. A Pathway along the Railway has been commenced. b, A + B Coys from U.12.D.7.9 to V.23.a.4.8. Several slight cases of gassing – A + D Coys moved to ROSE CAMP and continued work as above.	W.P.L.
	28th			W.P.L. note O.O. N⁰ 25
	29th		The Shelling in ROSE CAMP has become very prevalent and it is impossible for the men to rest. C Coy cleaned the BROOMBEEK from W.16.c.3.8. to NEVS cross Roads	W.P.L.
	30th		The Forward Companies hutted to BOESINGHE CAMP forbidden before	W.P.L.

Transport Officer.

The 1st and 2nd Line Transport will proceed to WHITE MILL, ELVERDINGHE to-morrow, via NORTHERN CHEMIN MILITAIRE (which starts at Cross Roads half mile N.W. of PROVEN and runs East to St SIXTE JUNCTION Sheet 28 N.W.) - St SIXTE JUNCTION - DE WIPPE CABT - ONDANK CABT - WOESTEN SWITCH.

All Transport will be clear of cross roads, half mile N.W. of PROVEN at 9-10 a.m.

West of the YSER CANAL 500 yards will be maintained between every 20 Vehicles.

The Transport of the 150th Brigade will pass the above Cross Roads at 9-0 a.m. and that of the 245 Machine Gun Coy. at 9-20 a.m.

W. F. Lamb

Capt. & Adjutant.
7th Bn. DURHAM Light Infantry.
(Pioneers).

23/10/17.

SECRET.

7th Bn. THE DURHAM LIGHT INFANTRY, (Pioneers).   23:10:17.

OPERATION ORDER NO. 24.

Reference map   1
HAZEBROUCK 5.a. 100,000

1. The Battalion less 1st and 2nd line Transport and Signal Section will leave PROVEN STATION to-morrow morning at 9-30.a.m. and will parade in full marching order on the main road outside of Camp at 9-30.a.m. in the following order:- "A" Coy, "C" Coy, "D" Coy, "B" Coy, Lewis Gun Detachment, Divisional Band, Bugle Band and Headquarters Details, with the head of the column opposite the entrance to the aerodrome.
On the march 200 yards will be maintained between Companies.

2. Baggage Wagons, Mess Cart, Field Kitchens, Maltese Cart and Band Wagon will be ready for removal at 7-45.a.m.

3. O.C. Coys, Officers, and N.C.Os i/c Details will render an exact marching out state to the Orderly Room at 7-30.a.m.

4. All men entraining will carry their blankets as no other transport for them is available.

5. The Signal Section will proceed by road to ELVERDINGHE leaving Camp at 6-30.a.m.

                                    (Sgd) W. P. Laing.
Issued at 7-30 p.m.   Capt. & Adjutant.

SECRET.

7th Bn. THE DURHAM LIGHT INFANTRY, Pioneers.   28:10:17.

OPERATION ORDER No 25.

"B" "C" and "D" Coys will parade in full marching order at half hour intervals between Companies, commencing at 2.p.m. and proceed to ROSE CAMP, G1.CENTRAL and after taking over the huts will proceed to work on RAILWAY STREET as yesterday.

Blankets in bundles of 10s, rations, officers' valises, and mess kit, will be collected by the Transport at 1-30.p.m.

1 Officer from "D" Coy, and 2 men from each of "B", "C", and "D" Coys will proceed to the Camp in advance of the Companies and allot the 20 vacant huts.

"A" Coy, will vacate the tents and take over equivalent huts.

1 Officer from "A" Coy will allot the huts to be taken over by "A" Coy, and report to this office as soon as possible the number of vacant tents and huts available for a Battalion of the N.Fs. arriving this afternoon.

"A" Coy, will arrange for these tents and huts to be guarded.

(Sgd) W. F. Laing.
Capt. & Adjutant.

SECRET.

The following alterations are made to Operation Order No 35.

1st para.	For "B", "C", and "D" Coys, read "A", "C", and "D" Coys.
3rd para	For "2 men from each of "B", "C", and "D" Coys" read "2 men from each of "A", "C", and "D" Coys"
4th para	delete.
5th and 6th paras	For "A" Coy" read "B" Coy".

28:10:17.

(Sgd) W. E. Lainy.
Capt. & Adjutant.

Army Form C. 2118.

7th Bn DURHAM LIGHT INFANTRY (PIONEERS)

VOLUME 31
OCTOBER 1917

WAR DIARY or INTELLIGENCE SUMMARY

(Erase heading not required.)

Instructions regarding War Diaries and Intelligence Summaries are contained in F. S. Regs., Part II. and the Staff Manual respectively. Title Pages will be prepared in manuscript.

Place	Date	Hour	Summary of Events and Information	Remarks and references to Appendices
In the Field	31st		The forward companies moved from BOESINGHE to a tent camp about B.18.c.6.5	W.P.R.

W. P. Laing
Captain & Adjutant
for Lt. Col. Commanding
7th Bn. The Durham
L.I. Regt. (Pioneers)
- Lt. Infty

7th Bn. The Durham Light Infantry. Pioneers.

Map Ref. LENS 11. Edition (2)   5th Oct. 1917

OPERATION ORDER No. 21.

1. The Battalion less 'B' Coy. will march to COURCELLES-LE-COMTE to-morrow Oct 6th. ROUTE:- Cross Country to cross roads North of the 'C' in HAMELINCOURT — COURCELLES-LE-COMTE.

2. Companies and Details will march independently, leaving their billets at the following times:— 'A' Coy, Div. Band, Signallers, Bugle Band 1-30 p.m.   'C' Coy. — 1. p.m   'D' Coy. — 2 p.m.   Lewis Gun Detachment, and Headquarters Details, — 2 p.m.
Companies will march with an interval of 100 yards, between each platoon until they reach the cross roads North of the 'C' in HAMELINCOURT. After that point, they will march closed up.
On arrival at COURCELLES, Companies and Details will be met by guides to conduct them to their billets.
The Transport will move independently.

3. Officers valises, mess gear, field kitchens and Maltese cart will be ready for removal at 12.30 p.m.

4. All billets and horse lines must be left clean, a certificate to this effect will be rendered to Orderly Room

Marching out states will be rendered to the Adjutant.

O.C. "C" Coy will arrange to leave guides to guide the incoming troops to the shelters on the NEUVILLE – VITASSE – WANCOURT ROAD.

                      Sgd. R. G. Macintyre
                          Capt. & Adjutant

Issued to:— Commanding Officer
            2nd in Command
            Adjutant
            Assistant Adjutant
            Medical Officer
            O.C. "A" Coy
            O.C. "C" Coy
            O.C. "D" Coy
            Lewis Gun Officer
            Quartermaster
            Transport Officer
            Regt. Sgt. Major
            War Diary
            File.

SECRET.
Copy No......15...
16th October 1917.

7th Bn. THE DURHAM LIGHT INFANTRY, (Pioneers) OPERATION ORDER No 22.

Ref. Map. 1/100,000.
Sheet 11.a. LENS.
SHEET 5.a. HAZEBROUCK.

1. The 149th Inf. Brigade Group will entrain at BAPAUME and MIRAUMONT on 18th October.

2. The Battalion will move to the entraining stations and entrain on 18th Octr.
(a) The Battalion less "B" Coy, and Transport will move to BAPAUME.
ROUTE:- GOMIECOURT-ARRAS-BAPAUME Road.
STARTING POINT:- Road on which O.M.Stores are, facing East.
ORDER OF MARCH:- Bugle Band, Divisional Band, "A","C", & "D" Coys.
TIME:- 9-10.a.m.
(b) "B" Coy will move to MIRAUMONT.
ROUTE:- ACHIET-LE-GRAND and ACHIET-LE-PETIT.
STARTING POINT:- Road junction 100 yards S. of COURCELLES on ACHIET-LE-GRAND Road.
TIME:- 12 noon.
(c) The Transport less 1 Cooker, 4 Tool Wagons and teams will move to BAPAUME.
ROUTE:- As for Battalion.
STARTING POINT:- Railway Crossing E. of COURCELLES.
TIME:- 8.a.m.
(d) 1 Cooker and 4 Tool Wagons and teams will move to MIRAUMONT.
ROUTE:- As for "B" Coy.
STARTING POINT:- Entrance to No 2.Div.Trains Camp (A.22.a.Sheet 57c.)
TIME:- 10-45.a.m.

3. The Transport will be loaded by evening of 17th Octr, with the exception of H. Q. Limber, the Valise Wagons and the Mess Cart. H.Q.Stores, Officers Valises and Mess Gear, will be collected by 6-30.a.m. on the 18th Octr. The R. S. M. will detail a loading party for these.

4. All tents, if dry weather continues, will be struck and handed in to the Quarter Master, by 4.p.m. 17th inst. He will return them, and any other AREA Stores, to the Town Major, and will send to the Adjutant a signed copy of all such.

5. All Companies will send to Orderly Room by 6.p.m. 17th inst, a complete marching out state of all men on strength of their Company, less Transport.
The Transport Officer will render a complete marching out state of the Transport, to Orderly Room by 6.p.m. 17th inst.

6. An Officer from each Company, and Transport Officer will attend at Headquarters at 6.p.m. 17th inst, to synchronize watches.

7. Billets and Horse lines will be left clean. O.C.Coys and Officers i/c Details will send a certificate to Orderly Room to this effect.

8. Full Marching Order will be worn.
Blankets and Waterproof sheets will be carried.
Water Bottles full.
Rations for 18th and 19th Octr. will be carried.
All Specialists and Details will march with their Companies.

9. The doors of covered trucks and carriages on right hand side of train will be kept closed when on the main line.

10. Piquets for each end of train will be detailed by O.C. "A" and "D" Coys at all stops to prevent troops leaving.

11. All animals will be watered before entraining.

12. (a) All trains consist of 1 Officers carriage, 17 flat trucks, and 30 covered trucks.
(b) Each flat truck will take an average of four axles.
Each covered truck will take forty men or 6 H.D. Horses or 8 L.D. Horses or Mules.

Sgd. J A Bell
Capt. & A/Adjutant.
7th Bn. The Durham Light Infantry, Pioneers.

SECRET.

7th Bn. The Durham Light Infantry, Pioneers.

Ref.Map.5.a. HAZEBROUCK. OPERATION ORDER No 23. 20:10:17.

1. The Battalion will move to PROVEN AREA to-day vide WORMHOUDT-HERZEELE-HOUTKERQUE.

2. The Battalion will parade to-day at 11.a.m. on the 2nd class road leading from RUBROUCK to WORMHOUDT in the following order:- Signallers, "B" Coy, "A" Coy, Divisional Band (with instruments) (Bugle Band (with instruments) "D" Coy, "C" Coy, Lewis Gun Detachment, Headquarters Details, 1st Line Transport, 2nd Line Transport, with the head of the column at point where two bye roads meet the 2nd class road ⅝ths mile So. of the E. in ERINGHEM.

3. Blankets in bundles of 10 will be ready for collection at 8-30.a.m. Companies and Details will provide loading parties.

4. Officers valises, Mess Kit, Stores, Packs belonging to Bandsmen, etc, will be ready for collection at 9.a.m. two men per Company will report to the Transport Officer at 9.a.m. to act as guides.

5. The Battalion will halt at 12-45.p.m. in order to have dinner. The march will be resumed at 2-15.p.m..

6. No man will fall out without written authority from an Officer. This authority will state destination of the Battalion.

7. SICK PARADE. All sick will parade at Headquarters in full marching order at 9.a.m.
   O.C. "D" Coy will detail one officer to attend Sick Parade and take charge of "Slow Party".

8. Lieut. A. H. Polge and 6 Signallers will rendezvous outside "A" Coys billet at 7-30.a.m. and proceed to Area Commandants Office PROVEN and report to Staff Capt. 149th Brigade for billeting. Three guides will meet the Battalion at HAUTERQUE.
   The Signallers will arrange for a bicycle to be there for Lt. Polge.

9. (a) Baggage wagons will report at 7.a.m.
   (b) Supply wagons will report at 8.a.m. loaded with rations for 21st.
   (c) Empty Baggage and supply wagons will return to H.Q. No 2 Train at PROVEN on completion of move.

(Sgd) W. F. Laing.
Capt.& Adjutant.
7th Bn. The Durham Light Infantry,
Pioneers.

Issued at 5-30.a.m.

WAR DIARY

of

7TH BATTN. DURHAM LIGHT INFANTRY

(PIONEERS).

VOLUME XXXII.

NOVEMBER 1917.

7th B. DURHAM LIGHT
INFANTRY (PIONEERS)

Army Form C. 2118.

WAR DIARY
or
INTELLIGENCE SUMMARY
(Erase heading not required.)

VOLUME 32
NOVEMBER

Place	Date	Hour	Summary of Events and Information	Remarks and references to Appendices
ELVERDINGHE	1st		During the night several enemy aircraft dropped between 150 and 200 bombs in and around the camp, resulting in CAPTAIN T.F. FORSTER being killed, CAPTAIN H. STEWART and LIEUT. W.A. RIDOUTT and 11 other ranks being wounded. The Companies rested today.	W.D.K.
	2nd		Work continued by all Companies on RAILWAY STREET as above	W.D.K.
	3rd		as above	W.D.K.
	4th		as above.	W.D.K.
	5th		The Companies rested. B Company moved from WHITE MILL CAMP to HULLS FARM	W.D.K.
	6th		The Battalion commenced work on forward roads in the C XIV Corps. The Shelling was	W.D.K.
	7th		extremely heavy today and the boys had several casualties - Vide note attached	W.D.K.
	8th		Work continued as above.	
HULLS FARM	9th		Headquarters moved to HULLS FARM.	W.D.K.
	10th 11 12 13		Work continued as above.	W.D.K.
	14th 15 16		Work continued on roads as above. 1 Company remains in camp each day. In this the difficulty in obtaining necessary material for the roads, work progresses very favourably.	W.D.K.
	20th		The Company in camp is employed in improving same - laying duck-boards -

Army Form C. 2118.

7:Bt DURHAM LIGHT
INFANTRY (PIONEERS)

WAR DIARY
or
INTELLIGENCE SUMMARY

VOLUME № 32
NOVEMBER 1917

(Erase heading not required.)

Instructions regarding War Diaries and Intelligence Summaries are contained in F. S. Regs., Part II. and the Staff Manual respectively. Title Pages will be prepared in manuscript.

Place	Date	Hour	Summary of Events and Information	Remarks and references to Appendices
HULLS FARM	21st to 25th		Work continued as above. A wet and dry canteen has been opened in Camp and a drying shed erected.	W.F.L.
	26th to 29th		Work continued as above.	W.F.L.
	30th		Companies remained in Camp taking trains to rejoin the Division in the EPERLEQUES Area.	W.F.L.

W.F.Laws
Captain & Adjutant
7: D.L.I. (Pioneers)

TABLE "A"

Date.	Unit in order of march.	Time to pass Starting Point.	Remarks.
Nov 11th.	447th Field Coy. R.E. To move under orders of O.C.Coy. and to be clear of the Starting Post-Railway Crossing, WATTEN Station by 8.45 a.m. Not to pass LED-ERZEELE Station before 11.0.a.m.		1. **Starting Point** Railway Crossing, WATTEN Station. 2. **Route.** ST.MOMELIN- LEDERZEELE St.- WARMARS CAPPEL. Not to pass LED- ERZEELE Station before 11.a.m.
	7th Durh.L.I. (Pioneers).	9.0.a.m	
	6th Durh.L.I.	9.5.a.m.	3. **Destination** ZERMEZEELE.
			4. **Billets.** 50th Divl.Train will arrange with area Commandant, ZERMEZEELE for accomodation.
			5. **Rations.** Transport will move from EPER- LECQUES Area with rations for consumption on 11th and 12th inst.
Novr 12th.	Order of march as above, except that No 3 Coy. 50th Div.Train will march first at 6.a.m	Under orders of B.T.O.	1. **Route.** WINNEZEELE- WATOU- POPERINGHE. To be East of WORMHOUDT- CASSEL Road by 9.a.m.
			2. **Destination.** BRANDHOEK.

To O.C. 7th D.L.I. Pioneer Battalion.

Reference C.E. XIX Corps No 2084.

According to the above letter your Battalion will work on the forward roads under our technical direction on and after the 6th November.

1. The roads in question is the main PILCKEN-LANGEMARCK POELCAPELLE road from a point half way between PERISCOPE HOUSE and IRON CROSS to the REDHOUSE.

2. 3 Companies to work daily, 1 Company to rest. This arrangement to hold good as long as the results are satisfactory, this might be plainly explained to the men.

3. Companies to meet the R.E. party on the work at the points mentioned in para 4 at 6.a.m. daily and work on a 4½ hour shift net until 10-30.a.m.

4. Road Sections and rendezvous as follows.
   (a) 1 Company at IRON CROSS for work on the road from the house at C.3.a.15.35. to the STEENBEEK + the road from IRON CROSS to VULCAN CROSS ROADS.
   (b) 1 Company at AU BONGITE for work on the road from the STEENBEEK to U.23.C.65.60. + from LANGEMARCK CROSS ROADS to U.29.a.50.85.
   (c) 1 Company at U.29.a.50.85 for work on the WHITE HOUSE and ALLOUETTE FARM roads + the road forward from U.23.c.65.60.

5. 1 Section of this Company will work directly with your Battalion. The O/C Section and his two Subalterns will be up daily and will keep in close touch with your officers.

6. A certain number of scrapers and brooms will be sent to you for use on sections A & B. Every man not taking up one of these should carry a shovel.
   A few picks only are required say 4%.

7. Arms have never been carried by us or parties working with us.

8. The road sections vary in unpleasantness, but one company resting every day will provide automatic relief, as each Company will work 3 days on one sector and then after resting relieve another Company on another sector.

9. The transport of material will be dealt with by this Company.

10. The work of each sector is roughly as follows:-
   (a) Widening of main road to 24 feet (34' between inside edge of drains) by Turkey walks,
      Cutting of drains.
      Removal of mud from sides of road.
      Maintenance.
   (b) Widening of main road as above.
      Drains.
      Removal of mud.
      Maintenance.
   (c) Chiefly maintenance and some slab laying.

(Sgd) H.E.B.Hickling.
Maj.
O.C.183 Coy.R.E.

SECRET.

7th Bn. Durham Light Infantry.

7th Bn. Durham Light Infantry and 7th Field Company R.E. will rejoin the 50th Division in the EPERLECQUES Area as follows :-

1st DECEMBER.

Transport will march as follows, 7th D.L.I. leading :-

Route. - DROMORE CORNER (A.18.d.3.8.) - INTERNATIONAL CORNER (A.9.a.2.4.) - Road in A.18.b. & c. - WORMHOUDT.

Time. - To reach DROMORE CORNER at 9.30 a.m.

Billets. - Apply Area Commandant WORMHOUDT.

2nd DECEMBER.

Transport will continue their march as follows :-

Destination. - 7th D.L.I. to GANSPETTE.) BILLETS
7th Fd. Coy. to WATTEN.) from Area
(Cmdt. WATTEN .)

Route. - ZEGGERS CAPPEL - BOLLEZEELE - WATTEN.

Time. - Reach WATTEN I p.m.

A distance of 200 yards will be maintained between Transport of Units.

(Sgd.) W. F. Laing.
Capt. & Adjutant.

30th November, 1917.

SECRET

7th Bn. The DURHAM LIGHT INFANTRY, Pioneers.   30th November
  O P E R A T I O N   O R D E R   No 24.   1917.

Referance Sheet 28 & 27. $\dfrac{I}{40,000}$

27.A.N.E.) $\dfrac{I}{20,000}$
27.A.S.E.)

1.   The Battalion will rejoin the 50th Division in the EPERLEQUES Area to-morrow and will be billetted in GANSPETTE.

2.   Busses to convey the Battalion will rendezvous at B.15.d.0.0. (sheet 28) facing N.W. at II.a.m. (about 500 yards S.E. of the Q.M. Stores on the ELVERDINGHE-BRIELEN Road).
      Companies and Details will arrive at the rendezvous at 10-55 a.m. independently. An Officer from each Company will report to the Adjutant that the Company has left Camp, and that the lines have been left clean.

3.   Mess Cart will be at the end of track A at 6.a.m. O.C.Coys will arrange to have surplus mess stores and kit there at that time.

4.   Horses for Cookers will arrive in Camp at 6.a.m.

5.   Separate orders have been issued to the Transport which will arrive at GANSPETTE at I.p.m. on the 2nd.

6.   Blankets in bundles of ten, officers valises, mess kit and dixies will be at the end of track A at 8-15.a.m. ready to be loaded on lorries. Companies will provide loading parties.

                              (Sgd)   W. F. LAING.
                                   Capt. & Adjutant.
                              for Officer Commanding.
Issued at 10-30 p.m.   7th. Bn. The Durham Light Infantry,
                                              Pioneers.

SECRET.

7th Bn. The Durham Light Infantry, Pioneers.
OPERATION ORDER No 24.   30th Novr 1917.

Reference Sheet 28 & 27. $\frac{1}{40,000}$

27.A. N.E. } $\frac{1}{20,000}$
27.A. S.E. }

1. The Battalion will rejoin the 50th Division in the EPERLEQUES Area to-morrow and will be billetted in GANSPETTE.

2. Busses to convey the Battalion will rendezvous at B.15.D.00 (Sheet 28) facing N.W. at 11.a.m. (about 500 yards S.E. of the Q.M.Stores on the ELVERDINGHE-BRIELEN ROAD).
   Companies and Details will arrive at the rendezvous at 10-55.a.m. independently. An officer from each Company will report to the Adjutant that the Company has left Camp, and that the lines have been left clean.

3. Mess Cart will be at the end of track A at 6.a.m. O.C. Coys will arrange to have surplus mess stores and kit there at that time.

4. Horses for Cookers will arrive in Camp at 6.a.m.

5. Separate orders have been issued to the Transport which will arrive GANSPETTE at 1.p.m. on the 2nd.

6. Blankets in bundles of ten, officers valises, mess kit and dixies will be at the end of track A at 8-15.a.m. ready to be loaded on lorries. Companies will provide loading parties.

Capt.& Adjutant.
for. Officer Commanding.
7th Bn. The Durham Light Infantry, Pioneers.

Issued at 10-30.p.m.

SECRET.

WAR DIARY

of

7th BATTALION   DURHAM.L.INFY (PIONEERS).

Volume no XXXlll.

DECEMBER 1917.

Army Form C. 2118.

WAR DIARY
or
INTELLIGENCE SUMMARY
(Erase heading not required.)

4th Bn THE DURHAM LIGHT INFANTRY (PIONEERS)

VOLUME N° 33 DECEMBER 1917

Place	Date	Hour	Summary of Events and Information	Remarks and references to Appendices
In the Field	1st		The Battalion moved to the EPERLECQUES area and were billetted in Farms at GANS PETIT- Headquarters being at 27.A.K.29.H.95.75.	Vide S.O. 24 attached. W.D.2.
	2nd		The 1st & 2nd Line Transport joined the Battalion – Today was spent with Company inspections and cleaning billets.	Copy order attached. W.D.2.
	3rd 4th 5th		Training has been carried out by Companies. The Divisional Band rejoined its unit. Training as above – The Battalion carried out a route march of 5 miles this morning. Small parties have been detailed to assist in erection of Horse lines for Divisional Train Machine Gun Corps & A.D.V.S.	W.D.2. W.D.2.
	6th 7th 10th 11th		Training as above. Training as above. Work continued erecting Stables	W.D.2.
	12th		The Battalion moved to new area in accordance with operation orders N°s 25, 26, 27 and entered tent camp at Sheet 28. T.2.D.6.2.	attached. W.D.2.
	13th		The 1st & 2nd Line Transport moved to Sheet 28. H.10.B Central Today was spent in spreading the Tents out which were very close together.	

Army Form C. 2118.

WAR DIARY
or
INTELLIGENCE SUMMARY

(Erase heading not required.)

4/5" THE DURHAM LIGHT
INFANTRY (PIONEERS)

VOLUME N° 33
DECEMBER 1917

Instructions regarding War Diaries and Intelligence
Summaries are contained in F. S. Regs., Part II.
and the Staff Manual respectively. Title Pages
will be prepared in manuscript.

Place	Date	Hour	Summary of Events and Information	Remarks and references to Appendices
In the Field	14th		The Lewis Gun Detachment relieved the guns of the 18th Middlesex. 2 men per gun are on MULETRACK from forward and are relieved every 48 hours. Work commenced on MULETRACK from DEVILS CROSSING forward to WINDMILL Sheet 28.D.26.B.9.4. Beechwood Slabs and steepers are used for this work. Three Companies are employed and the fourth Company works on the Camp.	No. 67.5 Division War Diaries
	15th 16th		Work as above. Work progresses slowly though owing to the difficulty in obtaining slabs. Small parties are working on a site for NISSEN HUTS beside the MENINGATE	No. 7.2
	17th 18th 19th		Work as above. The Mule Track is completed to D.21.D.15.20.	No. 7.1
	20th 21st 22nd		Work as above. The Track is completed to D.21.D.47.30.	No. 7.4
	23rd		Church Parades were held in Camp today. B Coy commenced erecting Nissen Huts but owing to the frosty state of the ground little progress was made.	No. 3.1.5
	24th 25th		Work continued as above. No work was done to day. Church Parade was held in the morning	No. 7.4 No. 7.R

2449 Wt. W14957/M90 750,000 1/16 J.B.C. & A. Forms/C.2118/12.

Army Form C. 2118.

WAR DIARY
or
INTELLIGENCE SUMMARY

(Erase heading not required.)

VOLUME No 33

DECEMBER 1918

Place	Date	Hour	Summary of Events and Information	Remarks and references to Appendices
In the Field	26th		Work as above. B Coy are working on Light Railway at D.21.A.	W.7.K / W.7.L
	27th		Work as above - The Mule Track is completed to D.21.D.65.50.	
	28th to 30th		Work continues as above. Lt J.E.SCOTT and small party have been engaged in clearing Pill Boxes in forward area - Progress is slow owing to the bad state of the boxes -	W.7.L
	31st		Work continued as above - The Mule Track is completed to D.22.C.20.95.	W.7.L

W. P. Laws
Captain and Adjutant,
7th Bn. Durham Light Infantry (Pioneers).

SECRET.

7th Bn. The Durham Light Infantry, Pioneers.   10:12:17.

OPERATION ORDER   No 26.

---

1. The 1st and 2nd Line Transport (less 3 Field Kitchens, 1 Baggage Wagon, 2 Water carts, and 9 Riders) will proceed to new area to-morrow.
   Starting point, Railway Crossing, WATTEN STATION, at 9.a.m.

2.   3 Field Kitchens.   6 H.D. Horses
     1 Baggage Wagon.   2 H.D. Horses
     2 Water Carts.   4 L.D. Horses
                                9 Riders.

   will arrive at ST OMER STATION at 9.a.m. on the 12th inst, and will detrain at HOPOUTRE. The N.C.O. in charge will have written instructions, stating destination.

3. Breast ropes to be provided by Transport Officer.

4. The N.C.O. proceeding from ST OMER on the 12th, will meet the Staff Captain, 151st Inf. Brigade, in the square, ST OMER to-morrow morning at 11 o'clock to be shown the approach to the station and entraining platform.

5. Baggage wagons will be returned to No 3 Coy, Divisional Train, at H.16.a.8.4. Sheet 28. on the morning of the 13th.

6. A distance of 100 yards will be maintained between every 6 vehicles.
   Between each Battalion Transport - 100 yards.

(Sgd) W. F. Laing.
Capt. & Adjutant.

50th Division.
G.X.3193/32

7th D. L. I. (Pioneers)

    Please arrange to relieve 6 Lewis Guns, of the 18th Middlesex Pioneers, employed on anti-aircraft work with, Divisional Artillery, on the 14th instant.

    An Officer should visit 18th Middlesex R.(Pioneers) at I.2.d.9.5. on the faternoon of the 13th inst to arrange all details of relief.

    Instructions regarding the duties of these Lewis Gun Detachments will be taken over from the 18th Middlesex R. (Pioneers) on relief.

(Sgd) E.C.Anstey,
Lt.Col.
General Staff,
50th Division.

11th December 1917.

Headquarters
    50th Division.

Reference your G.X. 3193/32 of 11:12:17.

6 Lewis Guns from this unit, have to-day relieved the Lewis Guns of the 18th Middlesex Pioneers employed on anti-aircraft work with Divisional Artillery.

The positions are:-
D.20.a.8.9
D.21.a.8.4.
D.14.a.8.4.
D.9.c.4.7.
D.16.a.5.9.
D.16.d.2.6.

(Sgd) W. F. Laing.
Capt. & Adjutant,
for Officer Commanding,
7th Bn. The Durham Light Infantry,
Pioneers.

14:12:17.

SECRET.

7th Bn. The Durham Light Infantry, Pioneers.
OPERATION ORDER No 27.   11:12:17.

Map Reference
Sheet 28.

1. The Battalion will proceed to forward area to-morrow morning entraining at WATTEN STATION by the 9-0 o'clock train, and will parade in full marching order (with steel helmets) on the main road at 7.a.m. in the following order:-
Signal Section, Drum & Bugle Band, "B" Coy, "A" Coy, "D" Coy, "C" Coy, Divisional Band, and Headquarters Details, with the head of the column facing East, at Headquarters.
    The Lewis Gun Detachment will join the column in rear of "C" Coy, as it passes their billet.
    1 Blanket per man will be carried.
    Leather jerkins will be worn under the equipment.
    Haversack rations will be taken.

2. Remainder of blankets in bundles of 10, officers valises, mess kit, and band boxes will be outside billets ready for collection at 6-0.a.m. Companies will arrange for blankets etc, to be placed on one dump xxx per company.

3. Two lorries will be at Q.M.Stores at 6.a.m.
    1 N.C.O. and 3 men from Divisional Band will accompany one lorry to WATTEN STATION with band boxes and act as unloading party. The bandmaster will arrange to meet this lorry at the Q.M.Stores.
    1 N.C.O. and 3 men from "B" Coy will meet the second lorry and collect stores from the Coys and Details Billets, and remain at WATTEN STATION as guard while the lorry makes a second journey.
    2 Signallers will act as guides to the drivers of the lorries.
    Companies and Details will arrange to leave loading parties for blankets in the event of the Coys parading before the lorries arrive. These parties will be in possession of written instructions to proceed immediately to WATTEN STATION after loading.

4. On detraining at BRANDHOEK the blankets on the men will be rolled in bundles of 10.

5. O.C. "B" Coy, will detail one officer to proceed to WATTEN STATION with the first lorry and superintend the loading of blankets &c., and obtain information from the entraining officer as to number of vans allotted to this unit.
    1 covered van on the train is allotted to this unit.

6. The cooks wagon will collect dixies and rations from "C" Coy, "B" Coy, and Details, and horses will collect Field Kitchens from "A" and "D" Coys at 6.a.m.

7. O.C. Coys and Details will hand to the Adjutant on parade a certificate stating that all billets occupied by them were left scrupulously clean.

8. O.C. "C" Coy will detail 1 N.C.O. and 6 O.R. to form a rear party, which will clean up all billets evacuated by this unit. This party will proceed to BRANDHOEK by the 10 o'clock train from WATTEN. An officer from the 6th D.L.I. will be in charge of all rear parties.

9. Destination.-
    Sheet 28, I.?.d.6.?.

                                    (Sgd) W. F. Laing.
                                        Capt. & Adjutant.

-SECRET-

WAR DIARY

of

7TH BATTALION DURHAM LIGHT INFANTRY (PIONEERS).

VOLUME XXXIV.

JANUARY, 1918.

50th Div — to shine
then 8th.

7ᵗʰ Bⁿ DURHAM LIGHT INFANTRY (PIONEERS)

Army Form C. 2118.

WAR DIARY
or
INTELLIGENCE SUMMARY
(Erase heading not required.)

VOLUME Nº 34

JANUARY 1918

Instructions regarding War Diaries and Intelligence Summaries are contained in F. S. Regs., Part II. and the Staff Manual respectively. Title Pages will be prepared in manuscript.

Place	Date	Hour	Summary of Events and Information	Remarks and references to Appendices
In the Field	1ˢᵗ to 3ʳᵈ		Work continued on mule track as before. 180 Belgians arrived this afternoon for work with this unit. Track completed to D.22.A.4.3	W.?.R.
	4ᵗʰ		We handed over all work to the 18ᵗʰ (Pioneer) Bⁿ The Middlesex Regiment this afternoon and took over their work. Our Six anti-aircraft Lewis guns were relieved by the Middlesex.	W.?.R.
	5ᵗʰ		Work commenced on Double Plank road from DEVILS crossing WINDMILL OBT and SEINE (Sheet 28) under C.E. VIIIᵗʰ Corps. The day was spent levelling the ground preparatory for laying sleepers.	W.?.R.
	6ᵗʰ		The 50ᵗʰ Division were relieved by the 38ᵗʰ Division today and we commenced wiring from C.23.D.6.4 to C.30.A.9.5 assisted by the 2ⁿᵈ N.HANTS Regᵗ. A double apron fence was laid and pickets for a second fence laid today.	W.?.R.
	7ᵗʰ		Wiring continued as above. We were assisted by a party of Belgian Engineers.	W.?.R.
	8ᵗʰ		Working as above. Strong posts at UHLAN & JASPER FARMS - O.29.B Central - and PLUM FARM C.24.C.5.4 wired. The 1ˢᵗ Bⁿ R.I.R. assisting in carrying material through	W.?.R.
	9ᵗʰ 10ᵗʰ		As above. The main belt of wire at C.23 - was laid	W.?.R.
	11ᵗʰ 12		As above. Work commenced with one Platoon draining Pill Box at C.23 D.1.2	W.?.R.

7th Bn DURHAM LIGHT INFANTRY (PIONEERS)

WAR DIARY or INTELLIGENCE SUMMARY

Army Form C. 2118.
Volume No 34
JANUARY 1918

Instructions regarding War Diaries and Intelligence Summaries are contained in F.S. Regs., Part II. and the Staff Manual respectively. Title Pages will be prepared in manuscript.

Place	Date	Hour	Summary of Events and Information	Remarks and references to Appendices
In the Field	13th		Work continued as above.	W.7.K
	14th		As above. - In addition M.G. Posts J.(23.A.6.2) and I.(C.23.A.5.4) were wired	W.7.K
	15th			
	16th		Owing to the inclement state of the weather no work was carried out to-day.	W.7.K
	17th		Wiring continued as above -	W.7.K
	18th		Work commenced clearing PICKLEHAUBE KEEP C.28.A.4.3.	W.7.K Return Strength W.7.K
	19th			
	20th		Work as above - The Transport moved to new area in accordance with orders. Vide letter to Transport Officer W.7.K. Vide O.O. N.29.	
	21st		The Bn: moved to new area. A Coy B Coy HdQrs are billeted in GONDARDENNE. C Coy in FRESINGHEM and D Coy in ESQUERDES.	W.7.K
	22nd to 26th		In new area. Time has been devoted to inspection and completing equipment.	W.7.K
	27th		The Battalion moved to YPRES AREA in accordance with attached O.O. No. 29. and new billets in camp at Sheet 28. I.2.D.9.8.	W.7.K
	28th			
	29th to 31st		Work commenced on forward area - 3 Coys working and 1 Coy resting - Work consist of maintaining artillery Road South between SEINE CROSS ROADS and PANET ROAD and to CHIN CORNER (D.16.B.65.10.) during the CREST LINE and reclaiming PILL BOXES.	W.7.K

Captains and Adjutants,
7th Bn. Durham Light Infantry (Pioneers).

S E C R E T.

TRANSPORT OFFICER.

1.   The 1st and 2nd line transport will leave present Horse Lines at 8-30 a.m. to-morrow, and move by road with the 447th Field Coy to the TILQUES Area.

2.   Transport of the 7th and 447th Field Coys and of the 7th Durham Light Infantry (Pioneers) will move by road on the 20th of January to WIZERNES. Transport will be staged in the ZEMERZEELE Area the night of the 20th-21st of January and in the RENESCURE Area the night of the 21st-22nd January, reporting for billets to the Area Commandant at ZEMERZEELE and RENESCURE respectively.

3.   Transport will proceed the 20th January to ZEMERZEELE by route POPERINGHE-STEENVOORDE-CASSEL; the 21st January to RENESCURE by route ZUYTPEENE and le NIEPPE; and the 22nd January to TILQUES Area by route ARQUES and BLENDECQUES.

4.   On arrival in the TILQUES Area the locations of the 7th Durham L.I. (Pioneers) will be arranged by the 50th Division (Headquarters WIZERNES).

5.   Particular attention is drawn to Battalion Order No X 43 of even date.

6.   Rations for 22nd inst for transport will be drawn by units at RENESCURE on 21st from R.S.O. at EBBLINGHEM.

Capt. & Adjutant,
7th Bn. The Durham Light Infantry,
Pioneers.

19:1:18.

Officer Commanding
                7th Bn. The Durham Light Infantry, Pioneers.

        Before you leave this area and I would like to express my appreciation of the good work done on the Army Battle zone by your officers and men whilst they have been working for me.

        I also wish to express my thanks for the helpful way in which you have carried on the work.

        Would you kindly let the officers and men know that I am pleased and satisfied with all that they have done.

                            (Sgd) G. F. Evans, Lt. Col. R.E.
                                C.R.E., 33rd Division.

20:1:18.

7th Bn. The Durham Light Infantry, Pioneers.   SECRET.
OPERATION ORDER No 28.   20:1:18.

Map Reference
5a HAZEBROUCK.
Sheets 28,27A.N.E.,27.A.S.E.

1.   The Battalion will move by rail to the FIEQUES area to-morrow, entraining at VLAMERTINGHE, detraining at WIZERNES.
2.   The Battalion will parade at 1-0 p.m. on the main road beside the Q.M.Stores in column of fours, facing West, in the following order:-
Signal Section-"A"Coy-"B" Coy- Drum and Bugle Band - "C" Coy - "D" Coy - Lewis Gun Detachment and Headquarters Details, with the head of the column at WELL Cross Roads.   The Band will march in front of the 3rd Company, and the Lewis Gun Detachment and H.Q. Details will march as a Company under the Command of an Officer to be detailed by O.C."D" Coy.
3.   "B" Company will detail an Officer to arrive at VLAMERTINGHE Station at 2 p.m. and act as entraining Officer.
4.   Officer's valises, Mess stores, Dixies, packs belonging to Drum & Bugle Band, and Blankets (in bundles of tens) will be at the Q.M.Stores at 8.45.a.m.   Companies and Details will provide loading parties.
5.   All water bottles will be filled.
6.   Lines will be left clean.
7.   Leather jerkins will be worn under the equipment.

                                Capt. & Adjutant,
                                7th Bn. The Durham Light Infantry,
                                        Pioneers.

SECRET.

7th Bn. The Durham Light Infantry, Pioneers.
OPERATION ORDER No.29.   26:1:18.

Ref. Maps-
Sheet 5a HAZEBROUCK.
Sheets 28, 27 A, S.E. and 36 D, N.

1. This Unit will relieve the 33rd Division (Pioneers) on 28th inst.

2. 'A' Coy., 'B' Coy., and Headquarters Details will parade in full marching order on the main WIZERNES - ARQUES Road at 7-30 a.m. on 28th inst., in the following order:- Signal Section, Drum and Bugle Band, 'A' Coy., 'B' Coy, and Details, with the head of the column at 'B' Coys Mess facing West.
'C' Coy and 'D' Coy will march independently and arrive at WIZERNES Station at 7-55 a.m.
Leather Jerkins will be worn under equipment.

3. 2 Field Kitchens, 2 Water Carts, 1 G.S. Wagon and 9 Chargers will arrive at WIZERNES Station at 6-0 a.m.

4. The following distances will be observed on the march:-
   Between Coys. - 100 yards.
   East of YPRES- 100 yards between platoons.

5. One Officer from 'D' Coy. will report to 150th Inf. Brigade H.Q. HALLINES at 3-0 p.m. to-morrow to synchronize watches.

6. Three lorries are allotted to this Unit and arrive at 150th Inf. Brigade H.Q. at 3-0 p.m. on 27th inst.
'D' Coy will detail one guide for one lorry which will remain outside 'D' Coys Mess on night of 27th, and convey blankets belonging to 'C' Coy and 'D' Coy.
'A' Coy will detail two guides to guide the remaining two lorries to the Quartermaster's Store.
Blankets, Valises, Mess Kit and Dixies will be collected at 6-0 a.m.
'D' Coy will detail one Officer to superintend the loading of 'C' and 'D' Coys Stores.
One C.Q.M.S., One Cook, and one batman from 'C' and 'D' Coys will accompany this lorry which will proceed to Q.M. Stores when loaded.
All Blankets &c from 'C' Coy will be placed on one dump and notification sent to O.C. 'D' Coy.
The Quartermaster will arrange for the collection of Blankets from the remainder of the Battalion.
The C.Q.M.S. from 'A' and 'B' Coys will accompany these lorries.

7. Certificates will be rendered to Orderly Room at 5-0 p.m. on 28th inst. that all Billets have been left clean.

- S E C R E T -
****

WAR DIARY

of

7TH BATTALION DURHAM LIGHT INFANTRY,
(PIONEERS)

VOLUME XXXV.

FEBRUARY, 1918.

Army Form C. 2118.

WAR DIARY
or
INTELLIGENCE SUMMARY
(Erase heading not required.)

7th Bn THE DURHAM
LIGHT INFANTRY
(PIONEERS)

VOLUME No 35
FEBRUARY 1918

Instructions regarding War Diaries and Intelligence Summaries are contained in F.S. Regs., Part II. and the Staff Manual respectively. Title Pages will be prepared in manuscript.

Place	Date	Hour	Summary of Events and Information	Remarks and references to Appendices
In the Field	1st		Work continued as above	
	2nd			
	3rd		As above - a party of 30 O.R.s worked on SIDING at SEINE D.16.C. (sheet 26)	A.?.C.
	4th		As above - The wiring of the MILITARY CREST is practically finished.	A.?.C.
	5th		As above - a party of 80 O.R. engaged burying cable at D.26.A.5.6	A.?.C.
	6th		Work as above. Division of Signals	A.?.C.
	7th		under Lieut. J.P. KNIGHT continue work reclaiming PILL BOXES.	A.?.K
	8th			
	9th		TURNING POINT at SEINE (D.16.D.2.6) completed today by 6 a.m. Church of England Parade Service held in Camp.	A.?.Y
	10th		Work on maintenance of ARTILLERY ROAD N°5 ¼, Duck Board Tracks' SEINE SIDING and CORPS TRAMWAY at HAALEN COPSE D.11.B.4.2	A.?.R
	11th		in progress.	
	12th		As above - The Signal Section are employed laboring cables in YPRES.	A.?.K
	13th			
	14th		As above	A.?.4
	15th			
	16th		Vide marching order attached	A.?.9

7ᵗʰ Bⁿ. THE DURHAM
LIGHT INFANTRY
(PIONEERS)

Army Form C. 2118.

VOLUME N° 35

FEBRUARY 1918

WAR DIARY
or
INTELLIGENCE SUMMARY

(Erase heading not required.)

Instructions regarding War Diaries and Intelligence Summaries are contained in F. S. Regs., Part II. and the Staff Manual respectively. Title Pages will be prepared in manuscript.

Place	Date	Hour	Summary of Events and Information	Remarks and references to Appendices
	11ᵗʰ to 20ᵗʰ		Work continued as above –	M.7.R.
	21ˢᵗ		All work in hand was handed over to 18ᵗʰ Bⁿ MIDDLESEX.	
	22ⁿᵈ		The Battalion moved to TILQUES area in accordance with attached Operation order N° 30	M.7.R.
	23ʳᵈ to 24ᵗʰ		In new area – The Companies are billeted in WIZERNES and WONDARDENNES. The Battalion Headquarters & Details in CONDARDENNES. The Battalion has been formed in accordance with new War Establishment	M.72.
	25 26 27		Training. All platoon practices for A.R.D. Completion	(48)
	28		Training carried on in billets –	(49)

George Nixon
2/Lt + a/Adjutant.
7th Bn. Durham Light Infantry

SECRET.

7th Bn. The Durham Light Infantry, Pioneers.

OPERATION ORDER No 30.

Map References.
5a HAZEBROUCK.
Sheets 28.27a.N.E.27.a.S.E.

1. The Battalion will move to TILQUES area on the 22nd inst, entraining at YPRES, at 2.p.m. detraining at WIZERNES at 5.p.m.
2. The 1st and 2nd line transport (less 3 Field Kitchens, 2 Water Carts, 1 G.S. Baggage wagon and 9 Riding Horses) will proceed by road on the 20th in accordance with Table "A" attached.
3. Remainder of transport will move by rail and will arrive at VLAMERTINGHE Station at 1.p.m. on the 22nd inst. Break ropes will be provided by the Transport Officer. On arrival at the Station the N.C.O. i/c will report to Capt. E.R.SALTONSTALL.M.C. 5th Yorks.Regt.
4. Lieut. S.PROBERT, Cpl Coupland and 9 other ranks from "B" Company will act as advance party. They will report to the entraining officer of the 151st Brigade at 12-30.p.m. on the 20th inst, at YPRES Station and travel by the 1 o'clock train. On arrival at WIZERNES they will report to the Staff Captain of the 150th Brigade, and take over billets occupied by the 18th Bn. Middlesex Regt. This party will carry rations for consumption on the 23rd.
5. 2nd Lieut. Colman will report to Capt.E.WATTS-MOSES, 4th E.Yorks.Regt, and will act as entraining officer. *at Ypres Station at 12-30pm on 22nd inst.*
6. The Battalion will parade in full marching order on the SAVILLE Road with the head of the column at junction of SAVILLE-POELJZE Road at 12-30.p.m. on the 22nd inst, in the following order:-
Signal Section, "A" Coy, "B" Coy, Drum & Bugle Band, "C" Coy, "D" Coy, Lewis Gun Detachment, and Headquarters Details.
7. Blankets in bundles of ten, Officers' Valises, Mess kit, Dixies etc., will be loaded by respective companies and details into Motor Lorries at Quarter Masters' Store by 8-30.a.m. on the 22nd inst.
C.Q.M.S., 1 Cook, and 1 batman from each Company will accompany these lorries by road.
These lorries (3) arrive in the square in YPRES at 7-30.a.m. 22nd inst, and will be met by 6 guides from "A" Coy. who will direct them to the Q.M.Stores.
8. Marching out states showing Nos of Officers and other ranks proceeding by train from YPRES will be handed into Orderly Room at 11-30.a.m. on 22nd.
9. Distances to be maintained on the march will be as under:- Between Coys - 100 yards. Between units and transport - 100 yards. A distance of 25 yards will be maintained between every 6 vehicles.
10. The Battalion will be in G.H.Q.Reserve from noon 22nd & will be ready to move by road or rail at 48 hours notice.
11. "A" Company will appoint an Officer to prepare a list of all stores in Camp to be handed over to the 18th Middlesex Regt. This list will be handed in to Orderly Room at 5.p.m. on 21st.

(Sgd) W.F.Laing
Capt & Adjutant.

19:2:18

SECRET.

TABLE 'A'

1. Starting Point   Cross Roads I.8.b.6.4.
2. Time.   8.4.a.m. on 20th inst.
3. Destination
   - on 20th – STEENVOORDE (via POPERINGHE).
   - on 21st – RUBROUCK   (via CASSEL (lower road)–BAVINGHOVE le MEPPE).
   - on 22nd – WIZERNES   (via ARQUES).

4. Orders for 2nd and 3rd day will be issued by D.T.O. March each day not to start later than 8-0.a.m.

5. HALTS.– on 20th will be:–
   1st halt 9-30.a.m. – 9-40.a.m.
   2nd halt 11-15.a.m. – 11.25.a.m.
   3rd halt 12-30.p.m. – 1.p.m. (feed and water)

6. 1 Mounted Orderly will report to the Brigade T.O. at 7-0.a.m. on 20th to arrange billetting.

7. The transport will march with the Brigade Group which is under the command of the Brigade Transport Officer – Capt. T.H.Hutchinson.

(Sgd) W. F. Laing.
Capt. & Adjutant.

SECRET.

7th Bn., THE DURHAM LIGHT INFANTRY, Pioneers.

WARNING ORDER.

1. The 1st and 2nd line transport (except as under) leave by road for WIZERNES on 20th inst.

2. Personnel leave by train from YPRES, approximate time of departure 1.p.m. arriving WIZERNES 4 p.m. 22nd inst.

3.   3 Field Kitchens.
       2 Water Carts.
       1 G.S. Wagon.
       9 Riders.

       leave by train from VLAMERTINGHE (approx. 4 p.m.) 22nd inst.

4. The 19th Bn. Middlesex Regt. Pioneers, will take over this present Camp, and it is the duty of all ranks to ensure that it is left clean.

5. Baggage wagons will be returned to this unit on the afternoon of the 19th inst.

6. Tool Wagons, Mess Cart, Maltese Cart &c will be loaded by 5.p.m. on the 19th inst.
All surplus kit will be sent by transport.

7. All tables, forms, Lamps F.S., Lamps R.R. will be handed over.

                          Capt. & Adjutant.
                          7th Bn. The Durham Light Infantry,
                                           Pioneers.

18:2:18.

50th Divisional Pioneers

7th BATTALION (Pioneers)

DURHAM LIGHT INFANTRY

M A R C H   1 9 1 8

Report on operations attached:

Army Form C. 2118.

7th Bn THE DURHAM LIGHT INFANTRY - PIONEERS

VOLUME No. 36

WAR DIARY or INTELLIGENCE SUMMARY

(Erase heading not required.)

MARCH 1918

Instructions regarding War Diaries and Intelligence Summaries are contained in F.S. Regs., Part II. and the Staff Manual respectively. Title Pages will be prepared in manuscript.

Place	Date	Hour	Summary of Events and Information	Remarks and references to Appendices
Field.	1		Three Companies billeted in Wizernes. Headquarters & detail in Confrebeault.	A.1.
	2		Pioneering & Infantry training carried out.	A.1.
	3		Training as above	A.1.
	4		Church Parade	A.1.
	5		Pioneering & Infantry training carried out as above.	A.1.
	6		As above. One Platoon of C Coy moved to TATINGHEM to work on "Lea Avenue"	A.1.
	7		Parade as above.	A.1.
	8		Standing by ready to move. "C" Coy proceeded to ARQUES Station to lose all transport of the 151st Bde groups	A.1.
	9		Entrained at ARQUES, Detrained at LONGEAU and marched to HAMELET (A & B Coy) & VAIRE-SOUS-CORBIE (Remainder of Bn) as per operation order attached.	A.1.
	10		Resting	A.1.
	11		Moved by march route to RAINECOURT (C Coy) and FRAMERVILLE (remainder of Bn) as per operation orders attached.	A.1.

2449 Wt. W14957/M90 750,000 1/16 J.B.C. & A. Forms/C.2118/12.

7B: THE DURHAM
LIGHT INFANTRY
(PIONEERS)

VOLUME N° 36

Army Form C. 2118.

MARCH 1918

WAR DIARY
or
INTELLIGENCE SUMMARY.

(Erase heading not required.)

Instructions regarding War Diaries and Intelligence
Summaries are contained in F. S. Regs., Part II.
and the Staff Manual respectively. Title pages
will be prepared in manuscript.

Place	Date	Hour	Summary of Events and Information	Remarks and references to Appendices
Field	12		Resting. One platoon of C Coy moved to HARBONNIÈRES to work under the C.R.E.	
	13		Training. Platoons practised the attack.	
	14		" " A Coy at bath.	
	15		Companies " "	
	16		" "	
	17		The Battalion moved to TERTRY vide O.O. No 34 attached.	A.9.X.
	18th		Battalion remained in Camp	
	19th		Battalion enforced digging small posts along the ridge through W.I. arc	
	20th			
	21st		6.20 The German offensive commenced this morning (21st) preceded by	A.9.X.
			Intense bombardment. The Battalion stood to arms at 4.30 am.	
	22nd		Vide Summary attached.	A.9.20
	to			
	31st			

W. F. Laing
Captain & adjutant
Lt Colonel
Commanding 7th Bn. Durham Light Infantry
(Pioneers).

7th Bn. THE DURHAM LIGHT INFANTRY, PIONEERS.

March 1918.

21st. Thursday. 21st   Warning telegram had been sent round by Division last night to expect a German Offensive commencing this morning, and as the Bombardment which had been continuing throughout the night increased to a great violence, the Battalion was ordered to "Stand To" at 4-30 a.m. At 9-0 a.m. as no orders were received the Companies proceeded to work on Strong Posts along the ridge W.1.a.&c (620). About 9-0 p.m. the Division passed through TERTRY to reinforce the front line.

22nd. Friday. 22nd   The Bombardment still continued with great violence and the Companies returned from work at midday. At 2-0 p.m. we received orders to proceed at once to CARTIGNY. On arrival we reported our location to Divisional Headquarters and awaited further orders.

23rd. Saturday. 23rd   At 4-0 a.m. orders were received to proceed at once to LE MESNIL and report to Divisional Headquarters. Instructions were issued for us to dig a line of posts from O.17.d.central to U.6.a.central refusing the right flank and to hold this line until orders were given to retire. In the meanwhile the Transport was despatched to BELLOY. As the enemy were still advancing the G.S.O. 1., ordered us to retire to BELLOY as the Infantry were withdrawn in front of us in good order.
    While the Battalion was resting along the road at VILLERS-CARBONNEL several E.A., flying low, fired machine guns at the traffic on the roads. We retaliated with rifle and machine gun and one machine was brought down. Just before moving off to BELLOY, Major G.D.R. Dobson and three men were wounded and two killed by H.E.

24th. Sunday. 24th   At 8-0 a.m. we received orders to take over part of the line on the Canal from ETERPIGNY to O.9.central to fill a gap caused by the 66th Division on our Left and the 8th Division on our Right. We arrived in position about 3 o'clock in the afternoon and throughout the night were much worried by our Howitzers firing short.

25th. Monday. 25th   At day break it was found that the enemy had pushed a patrol across the Canal on our Right and had a machine gun in position in ETERPIGNY firing from the flank. The Battalion on our Right had been relieved during the night and the post holding the Bridge over which the patrol had advanced had evidently been overlooked. About 7-0 a.m. Captain Thompson, commanding the Company on the right, reported the enemy on our side of the Canal in large numbers and that as his Right flank was in the air he could not hold on. Orders were thereupon given to withdraw. The Battalion withdrew, in order, over the ridge and took up position along a line through O.13.a.central and O.7.d.central where they met the 5th D.L.I. coming up to deliver a counter-attack. During the morning 150 men were sent up to reinforce the 5th D.L.I. About 5-0 p.m. the Companies were sent forward to occupy a line running through the centre of O.7.b. which was held until orders were given to withdraw to ESTREES at 7-30 p.m.

7th Bn. THE DURHAM LIGHT INFANTRY, PIONEERS.

(2)   March 1918.

26th. Tuesday. 25th   The Battalion took up position on the North of ESTREES shortly after midnight from about N.25.a.9.9. to N.19.central. About 9-0 a.m. the enemy were reported to be advancing in large numbers and the 149th Brigade (Infantry) sent orders to withdraw at 10-0 a.m.. The Battalion withdrew to a line through X.11.a.central at 2-0 p.m. "A" and "B" Companies were then ordered to attack FRAMERVILLE, while the 5th N.F's delivered a counter-attack on the Left of the village. The Companies forced their way through the village twice, but owing to the commanding position held by the enemy with his machine guns, it was impossible to remain and were compelled to withdraw to the line about 500x immediately South of the village. At dusk all troops under the 149th Brigade were withdrawn and we occupied posts immediately on the South side of the Main Railway about X.25.b.2.2.

27th. Wednesday. 27th   Heavy fighting was in progress at ROSIERES on our Right front and about mid-day we were given orders to retire on to the BAYONVILLERS - GUILLAUCOURT line. On arrival at GUILLAUCOURT, as the enemy had been repulsed we were ordered to line the Sunken Road through W.18.a.&c. Towards nightfall we were ordered to push forward and occupy the VAUVILLERS Ridge which was done with little or no opposition.

28th. Thursday. 28th   We were relieved this morning and on taking up a position along the Sunken Road in Support at 5-0 a.m. orders were received to withdraw to CAIX. The Division took up position in front of CAIX and this Unit occupied a Sunken Road N.E. of CAIX. Towards mid-day the position grew critical as both flanks had retired, but the Battalion held on until the order was given to withdraw at 3-30 p.m. and a position was taken up on the ridge immediately West of CAIX. The French who had been coming up during the day were holding a portion of the front and the Battalion withdrew about 6-0 p.m. and proceeded to MOREUIL and "A" Company proceeded to BOVES.

29th. Friday. 29th   About 1-30 a.m. a man came to Headquarters and said all troops had to clear out of the village at once as the enemy were close at hand. This subsequently turned out to be the work of a spy. The remainder of the Battalion (about 60 strong) cleared out of the village and were collected together and sent into the line with the remnants of the Division near the X Roads South of DEMUM.

30th. Saturday. 30th   The Battalion (less the above 60 men under Captain Dickson) collected in BOVES and marched to SANS-EN-AMIENOIS.

31st. Sunday. 31st   The Battalion marched to SALEUX for entrainment to RUE.

7th Bn. The Durham Light Infantry, Pioneers.
WARNING ORDER.
_____

In the event of this unit having to entrain at short notice.

"A" Company, 1 Cooker and team will entrain at ARDWES with the 1/1st (Northern) Field Ambulance and one Company from 5th Bn. The Durham Light Infantry. The remainder of the Battalion will travel on a separate train from the same station.

The route to the station will be via WESTOVE.

(Sgd) W. F. Laing.
Capt. & Adjutant.

7th Bn. The Durham Light Infantry. Pioneers.

OPERATION ORDER No 81.

8:3:18.

Map References.
Amiens 17.
Sheets 27.A.S.E. 36.D.N.E.

The Battalion will entrain at ARQUES Station to-morrow detraining at LONGEAU.

"A" Company, one cooker and teams, will move independently to ARQUES Station, Route via GONDARDENNE-WESTOVE-. Train departs 8-27.a.m. "A" Company should arrive at Station at 7.a.m.

Remainder of Battalion will parade in the following order on WIZERNES-GONDARDENNE Road, with the head of the column, facing East at F.4.C.4.9. at 8.a.m. to-morrow.

Signal Section, Drum & Bugle Band, "B" Coy, "C" Coy, Lewis Gun Detachment & Details.

Dress:- Full Marching Order for all Parades.

One blanket per man will be carried. Water bottles must be carried full.

Transport will move off as 1½ hours before the Battalion and will take the same route as "A" Coy.

O.C. "B" Coy will detail one officer and 50 other ranks to proceed with Transport. They will act as loading party.

O.C. "C" Coy will detail 1 Officer and 50 other ranks to act as detraining party on arrival at destination.

Breast ropes for horse trucks will be supplied by Transport Officer. Rope for lashing vehicles on the flat trucks will be provided by Railway Authorities.

All doors of covered trucks and carriages on the right hand side of the train, when on the main line, must be kept closed.

Transport Officer will arrange for watering of horses before entraining, and also at hours halt at TATNQUES, 1st R.T.O there reports to O.C. Train that there is time.

ADVANCE PARTY.- Lieut. S. Probart, Cpl Coupland and one Signaller, with bicycles, will entrain at ARQUES Station with the 5th Bn D.L.I. at 2-27.a.m. to-morrow.

They should be at the Station at 2.a.m.

On arrival at destination the party will report to The Administrative Commandant, VILLERS-BRETONNEUX for instructions.

They will meet the Battalion on detraining (approx. 6 hours later than themselves) and act as guides.

Blankets in bundles of ten will be ready for collection at 6.a.m.

Officers valises and mess gear will be ready for collection at 6.a.m.

O.C. "A" Company will leave two men to act as guard over blankets etc. They will come on with "B" Company.

Company Commanders, Transport Officer, Lewis Gun Officer, and Officers and N.C.Os. in charge of Details, will render to Orderly Room by 8.p.m. to-day 8th inst. complete marching out states, shewing number of officers and men, horses, G.S.Wagons, Limbered G.S.Wagons, and 2 wheeled vehicles, and bicycles.

Each portion of Limbered G.S.Wagons will be counted as a 2 wheeled vehicle on the state.

Billets will be left in a clean state, and a certificate to this effect will be handed to the Adjutant on parade.

2nd Lieut. & A/Adjutant.
7th Bn. The Durham L.I. (Pioneers).

7th Bn. The Durham Light Infantry _ Pioneers.

OPERATION ORDER No 32.

Map reference
Sheet 17. AMIENS.
1/100,000.

The Battalion will move by march route to-morrow, 11th March to FRAMERVILLE and RAINECOURT.

Divisional Band, Bugle Band, "C" Coy, Lewis Gunners, H.Q.Details and Transport will parade at 8.a.m. on VAIRE-HAMELET Road, head of column 500 yards from Church in VAIRE facing South West.

"A" and "B" Coys, 2 Cookers, Valise Wagons and Mess Cart will be paraded ready to join column when passing through HAMELET.

Dress:- Full marching order.

Soft caps will be worn, steel helmets on valise, leather jerkins will be rolled in waterproof sheet and carried on top of the valise.

Water bottles will be filled.

All blankets will be rolled tight and neatly in bundles of ten and ready for collection at 7-30.a.m.

Each Company and Details will form a central dump.

Officers' valises and Mess Gear will be ready for collection at 7.a.m.

Transport Officer will make all necessary arrangements.

Sgt McGahan will detail 2 Signallers to meet three lorries at 151st Infantry Brigade Headquarters in the Square, CORBIE at 7-30.a.m. and will direct them to the Q.M.Stores HAMELET.

The Quarter Master will arrange for collection of all Band gear and blankets on arrival of lorries.

All Companies and Details will supply their own loading parties for blankets etc.,

TRANSPORT. Intervals of 25 yards will be maintained between each group of six vehicles.

Lorries must be loaded within 30 minutes of reporting and not kept waiting unnecessarily.

Slow party will parade under Lieut.A.E.HOPSON at 8.a.m. at the Church in HAMELET and will proceed direct to new area.

[signature]

2/Lieut. & A/Adjutant.
Lth Bn. The Durham Light Infantry,
Pioneers.

10:3:18.

Issued at 2.a.m. 11th inst.

7th Bn. The Durham Light Infantry, Pioneers.

Warning Order No 33.

The Battalion will probably move to the 19th Corps area to-morrow, 16th March, for work.

Personnel by Bus.
Transport by Road.

Company tool wagons and Lewis Gun Limbers will be packed to-day.

15:3:18.
(Sgd) C. Dixon.
2/Lieut. & A/Adjutant.

7th Bn. The Durham Light Infantry, Pioneers.

OPERATION ORDER No 34.   16:3:18.

Reference Map
AMIENS 17   (Sheet   )
ST QUINTIN.13.(62.D.S.E.)

   The Battalion less one platoon (in Command of 2nd Lieut. T.C.Squance) will move from PROYART Area to TERTRY to-day the 16th March by lorries.
Signallers, Bugle Band, "A" Coy, "B" Coy, Lewis Gun Detachment and Headquarters Details will parade on FRAMERVILLE-VAUVILLERS Road, head of the column at cross roads in FRAMERVILLE facing North at 8-15.a.m.
DRESS:- Full Marching Order, Water Bottles filled, Leather Jerkins will be rolled in waterproof sheets and carried on top of valise.
Soft caps will be worn, Steel Helmets fastened on valise.
"C" Company will be paraded on FRAMERVILLE-RAINECOURT Road, head of column at Folk roads R.33.D.7.4. facing N.E. and will join Battalion when it passes through RAINECOURT.
"A" Coy, "B" Coy and all Details Blankets, in bundles of ten, dixies and tea ration, will be dumped at Cross Roads FRAMERVILLE by 8.a.m.
"C" Coys at R.33.D.7.4. by 8.a.m.
Officers' Valises and Mess Gear will be ready for collection at 7-30.a.m.
Sgt McGahan will detail an Orderly to report to Orderly Room at 8-30.a.m.
Transport will move by road and will proceed direct to TERTRY and will parade as soon as ready.
ADVANCED PARTY.- Lieut.Probert, Cpl Coupland and 4 Signallers with cycles will meet at FRAMERVILLE Cross Roads at 6.a.m. and will report to Area Commandant TREFCON who will allot billets.
The Platoon under the command of 2nd Lieut. T.C.Squance will remain at HARBONNIERES for work under C.R.E. until further orders.
BILLETS.- Billets will be left in a clean and sanitary condition.
Marching out states will be handed to the Adjutant on Parade.

          Geo Rinson

          2nd Lieut.
Issued at 2.a.m.   A/Adjutant.

INSTRUCTIONS FOR MOVE.

1. Particular attention will be paid to discipline on the march, embussing and debussing, entraining and detraining.
2. On arrival at NAMETZ the Battalion will be told off from front to rear in parties of 25 for each bus, and 20 for each lorry.
3. 3 buses occupy 80 yards of road space.
4. On arrival at the station, the Battalion will entrain as soon as possible after the trucks are allotted.
5. All doors of covered trucks and carriages on the right side of the train, when on the main line, will be kept closed.
6. Each company will detail an N.C.O. whose duty it will be to prevent troops detraining without permission.

(Sgd) W. F. Laing.
Capt. & Adjutant.

(2)

Operation Order No. 29. contd.

8. One Officer from 'C' Coy will report to Major J. PLUMER, 5th Bn. D.L.I. (Brigade Entraining Officer) at WIZERNES Station at 7-30 a.m. on 28th inst, and act as entraining officer.

9. An advance party from 18th Middlesex (Pioneers) will arrive at 150th Inf. Brigade H.Q. at 10-30 a.m. on 27th inst, and will be met and accommodated by 'B' Coy.

10. The remainder of the Transport will arrive at Road Junction - X.3.B.7.8. at 9-35 a.m. on 27th inst, and march under Brigade Transport Officer.
The Transport Officer will send a mounted orderly to xxxxxxxxxx report to the Brigade Transport Officer at this point at 8-0 a.m.

11. Night of 27/28th Jany. will be spent at OUDEZEELE.
Billets from Area Commandant, OUDEZEELE.
The Horse Standing of the 18th Middlesex (Pioneers) will be taken over on arrival in new area on 28th inst.

12. The route will be:-
St. MARTIN-au-Laert.
St. MOMELIN.
LEDERZEELE Station.
CASSEL.
STEENVOORDE.
POPERINGHE.

13. The following distances will be observed on the march:-
100 yards between Units Transport.
25 yards between each section of 6 vehicles.

W. F. Lamé

Capt. & Adjutant.
7th Bn. The Durham Light Infantry,
(Pioneers).

50th Divisional Pioneers

1/7th BATTALION

DURHAM LIGHT INFANTRY (Pioneers)

APRIL 1918.

WAR DIARY.

OF

7TH Bn. D. L. I. (PIONEERS)

for month of

APRIL 1918.

VOLUME XXXVII

****

7: B: T.F. DURHAM   VOLUME N° 37
LIGHT INFANTRY (PIONEERS)   Army Form C. 2118.

WAR DIARY
or
INTELLIGENCE SUMMARY.
(Erase heading not required.)

APRIL 1918

Place	Date	Hour	Summary of Events and Information	Remarks and references to Appendices
In the Field	1st		Arrived at BERNAY near CRECY and were billetted in Farm.	W.9.2.
	2nd		Time devoted to refitting and reorganizing.	W.9.2.
	3rd			W.9.2.
	4th		The Battalion moved by Bus to BEUVRY (Sheet 36) vide O.O. R° 35 attached and were billeted in LE QUESNOY	W.9.2.
	5th		Re-equipping of the Battalion in progress	W.9.2.
	6th			
	7th		Battalion moved to ROBERMETZ	W.9.2.
	8th		Billets ROBERMETZ.	
	9th		An enemy offensive commenced this morning and MERVILLE and ESTAIRES were heavily bombarded — B Coy were engaged clearing the debris from the roads in the former and C Coy in the latter. A Coy proceeded this morning to reinforce the 6th D.L.I. in front of LESTREM, the remainder of the Bn. Stood to arms.	W.9.2.
	10th		C Coy were engaged this morning digging a line of posts on either side of the main NEUF BERQUIN — ESTAIRES R⁰ and B Coy a line of posts in front of MERVILLE. As the day progressed the enemy pushed on his attack and all Coys were in close touch with the enemy.	W.9.2.
	11th			

7th B. THE DURHAM LIGHT INFANTRY (PIONEERS)

VOLUME No 37

Army Form C. 2118.

Instructions regarding War Diaries and Intelligence Summaries are contained in F.S. Regs., Part II. and the Staff Manual respectively. Title pages will be prepared in manuscript.

WAR DIARY
or
INTELLIGENCE SUMMARY.
(Erase heading not required.)

APRIL 1918

Place	Date	Hour	Summary of Events and Information	Remarks and references to Appendices
In the Field	11th		(Continued) Towards nightfall the line fell back N.W. of NEUF BERQUIN	W.D.Y.
	12th		The 5th Division relieved the Division this evening and the Battalion collected at LA MOTTE and occupied the out houses of the CHATEAU.	W.D.Y.
	13th		About 5.0 a.m. the CHATEAU was heavily shelled for quarter of an hour resulting in several N.C.O.'s & men being killed & wounded. The Bn. were withdrawn to billets at J.1.D.5.1.	W.D.Y.
	14th to 17th		The Bn. was engaged digging & wiring lines at J.5.6.11 & 12	W.D.Y.
	18th		The Bn. moved by Route March to MAMETZ area and were billeted in WARNE H.13.A. (Vide O.O. N° 37)	W.D.Y.
	19th		Inspections were held today & deficiencies accounted for	W.D.Y.
	20th		The Bn. was inspected this morning by the Divisional General Major General H.C. Jackson D.S.O. - The G.O.C. thanked all ranks for the work they had done during the last two battles and said how proud he was to have such a Pioneer Battalion in his Division	W.D.Y.

7th Bn. THE DURHAM
LIGHT INFANTRY (PIONEERS)

VOLUME N° 37
Army Form C. 2118.

WAR DIARY
or
INTELLIGENCE SUMMARY.
(Erase heading not required.)

APRIL 1918

Instructions regarding War Diaries and Intelligence
Summaries are contained in F. S. Regs., Part II.
and the Staff Manual respectively. Title pages
will be prepared in manuscript.

Place	Date	Hour	Summary of Events and Information	Remarks and references to Appendices
In the Field	21st		Divine Services here held today.	W.9.L
	22nd		Training commenced this morning in accordance with attached programme.	W.9.L
	23rd am to 25th		Training as above	W.9.L
	26th		The Battalion moved to new area	Vide O.O. N°39.
	27			
	28		The Battalion arrived at VEZILLY - detraining at FERE (SOISSONS 22)	W.9.L
	29		The men are billetted in huts. Inspections were held today.	W.9.L
	30		Company Comm breed train up today. Pass levis laid on musketry	W.9.L

W.9.Lewis
Captain tadjutant
for
Lt. Colonel,
Commanding 7th Bn. Durham Light Infantry
(Pioneers).

7th Bn. The Durham Light Infantry, Pioneers.
OPERATION ORDERS.   No 37.   17:4:18.

      The Battalion will move to the MAMETZ Area to-morrow morning and will parade in Fighting Order on the main road at 10.a.m. in the following order:-
Signal Section, "A" Coy, "B" Coy, "C" Coy, Lewis Gun Detachment, Headquarters Details, with the head of the column at the road junction J.7.b.05.90.
      The transport will not pull out into the main road until the rear of the column moves off.
      All blankets, packs, and camp kettles will be handed into the Quarter Masters Store at 8-30.a.m.
      Officers valises and mess kit will be ready for collection at 9-0.a.m.
      Sick Parade will be held at 8-15.a.m. at Q.M.Stores. All men will parade in Fighting Order.
      Particular attention will be paid to march discipline. When marching at east rifles will be slung on the same shoulder, the change will be taken from the head of the column.

(Sgd) W. F. Laing,
Capt: & Adjutant.

7th Bn. The Durham Light Infantry, Pioneers.

OPERATION ORDER No. 36.

6/4/18.

The Battalion will entrain to-morrow at VENDIN for ESTAIRE Area. (Time will be notified later.)

Packs (with blankets <u>folded</u> under the supporting straps) and Dixies will be taken to the Q.M. Stores at 7-30 a.m. to-morrow. Surplus blankets will be rolled in bundles of 10.

The Battalion will parade in Fighting Order with waterproof sheets on the haversack. Haversack rations will be carried.

Lieut. Probert and 6 Buglers will proceed with Motor Lorries, leaving Q.M. Stores at 8-0 a.m. and act as Billeting Party.

Time for valises and Mess kit will be notified later.

1 Cook per Company and 1 Cook for Details will proceed with the Lorries.

The Divisional Band will parade with the Battalion.

(Sgd) W. F. Laing,
Capt. & Adjutant.

6/4/18 10-0 p.m.

7th Bn. The Durham Light Infantry, Pioneers.

OPERATION ORDER No. 35.   3:4:18.

The Battalion will parade in full marching order to-morrow morning at 9-45 a.m. on the main road in the following order, "A" Coy, "B" Coy, "C" Coy, Divisional Band, with the head of the column at the X Roads beside Headquarters Mess facing North. All Details will parade with their Companies.

No kit of any sort will be carried in the Busses.

On arrival at the rendezvous the Battalion will be distributed along the right hand side of the road as follows:-
6 Groups (of 25 men under an Officer) on each 50 yards of road space.

Vehicles are not reserved for Officers only. Officers will be distributed among the vehicles forming the Convoy.

All valises, mess kit and blankets in bundles of 10 will be ready for collection on the Main Road at 8-0 a.m. A small loading party will remain at Dump until stores are collected. These parties will be in full marching order ready to march off with the Battalion.

Capt. & Adjutant.

3:4:18.

SECRET.

7th Bn. The Durham Light Infantry, Pioneers.
OPERATION ORDER No 33.

1. The Battalion will entrain for new area at PERNES on 27th inst, and will parade to-morrow 26th inst at 5-30.p.m. on the main WARNE-RINCQ road in the following order:-
"A" Coy, Divisional Band, "B" Coy, "C" Coy, Lewis Gun Detachment, & Headquarters Details, with the head of the column facing South at the road junction 200 yards South of "B" Coys Officers Mess.
   The Battalion will then proceed to MAMETZ for embussing.
Dress:- Full marching order - 1 blanket and steel helmet will be carried under the supporting straps. Water Bottles will be filled.

2. The first and second line transport will arrive at PERNES Station at 10-45.p.m. to-morrow, and will be ready to move off at 1-30.p.m. to-morrow.

3. Lieut. S. Probert and ~~six Signallers~~ five Buglers with bicycles will form an advance party and proceed with the first train, leaving PERNES at 9-46.a.m. to-morrow. This party will leave cross roads beside transport lines at 5-30.a.m. and carry rations for consumption up to and including 29th inst.

4. An Officer from "B" Coy will report to the 149th Inf. Brigade embussing Officer at the cross roads MAMETZ at 7-30.p.m. to-morrow.
   Above Officers will report to the Adjutant to-morrow morning at 10 o'clock for further instructions.

5. All billets must be left in a thoroughly clean and sanitary condition.

6. The minimum number of camp kettles will be kept back for tea. These will be collected by motor lorry at 4-15.p.m.

N. F. Laing

Capt. & Adjutant,
7th Bn. The Durham Light Infantry
Pioneers.

25:4:18.

7th Bn. Durham Light Infantry - Pioneers

Weekly Training Programme.

Date	Time From	To	Place	Nature of Training	Remarks
1918 April 22	8.30 a.m	12.30 p.m	H.7.c.6.5.	Physical training, Musketry, Arm Drill, Close Order Drill, Company Drill.	In addition
" 23	do	do	do	Physical training, Open Order Drill, Arm Drill, Gas Drill.	Riding Lessons for all Officers
" 24	do	do	do	Physical training, Gas Drill, Wiring, Arm Drill.	training of NCOs under RSM
" 25	do	do	do	Attack Flagged by boys.	Officers lectured on
" 26	do	do	H.7.c.6.5.	Attack R⁻	Topography and
" 27	do	do	do	Summary of weeks work by C.O. = Battalion Drill	compass bearing.
" "	afternoon		do	Sports.	

Box 2823

7th Bn Durham Light Infantry

MAY & JUNE 1918

WAR DIARY

SECRET.

WAR DIARY

OF

7th DURHAM LIGHT INFNATRY (PIONEERS)

VOLUME XXXVIII

May, 1918.

WAR DIARY
or
INTELLIGENCE SUMMARY

(Erase heading not required.)

7th Bn. THE DURHAM LIGHT INFANTRY (PIONEERS)

Army Form C. 2118.

Place	Date	Hour	Summary of Events and Information	Remarks and references to Appendices
Field	1/5/18		Continued training at VEZILLY	A244/13
	2/5/18		as above	A242/13
	3/5/18		as above	A249/13
	4/5/18		as above	A244/13
	5/5/18		Battalion moved to ROMAIN	A244/13
	6/5/18		Battalion moved to dug-outs at CENTRE DEVREUX. Transport moved to CONCEVREUX	A244/13
	7/5/18		One Platoon "A" Coy moved to BEAUREPAIRE and one Platoon "A" Coy moved to LA SAPINIERE for work on 60 cm Railway	A244/13
	8/5/18		2 Platoons "B" Coy moved to R.C. P.met for work and remainder of "B" Coy moved to CHAMP BASILE for work on roads.	A244/13
	9/5/18		2 Platoons "A" Coy moved to dug-outs at CRAONNE for work on dug-outs and trenches. C Coy attached to 151st Infty Brigade for work in line	A244/13
	10/5/18		Battalion continued work	A244/13
	11/5/18		as above	A244/13

Army Form C. 2118.

WAR DIARY
or
INTELLIGENCE SUMMARY

(Erase heading not required.)

Instructions regarding War Diaries and Intelligence Summaries are contained in F. S. Regs., Part II. and the Staff Manual respectively. Title Pages will be prepared in manuscript.

Place	Date	Hour	Summary of Events and Information	Remarks and references to Appendices
Field	12/5/18		Battalion continued work. Headquarters moved to dugouts near MONACO Dump	A241/3
	13/5/18		Battalion continued work	A241/3
	14/5/18		Battalion continued work	A241/3
	15/5/18		as above	A241/3
	16/5/18		as above	A241/3
	17/5/18		as above	A241/3
	18/5/18		as above	A241/3
	19/5/18		as above	A241/3
	20/5/18		as above	A241/3
	21/5/18		as above	A241/3
	22/5/18		as above	A241/3

Army Form C. 2118.

WAR DIARY
or
INTELLIGENCE SUMMARY
(Erase heading not required.)

Place	Date	Hour	Summary of Events and Information	Remarks and references to Appendices
Field	23/5/18		Battalion continued work. C" Coy went into line with 8th D.L.I.	appx/3
	24/5/18		as above.	appx/3
	25/5/18		as above.	appx/3
	26/5/18		as above.	appx/3
	27/5/18		At 1 am the enemy commenced a heavy bombardment, the area in which the Battalion were situated was subject to severe shelling – the bombardment was followed by the enemy attacking in great force. A Company withdrew, the orders of the 150th Bgde. B & C Coys 2 Platoons of B Coy were ordered to proceed forward to help retain & under supervision to transport. The enemy advanced and all available men of the Battalion held strongpoints in the vicinity of Monaco.	
	28/5/18		The Battle continued	appx/3 appx/3

2449 Wt. W14957/M90 750,000 1/16 J.B.C. & A. Forms/C.2118/12.

WAR DIARY or INTELLIGENCE SUMMARY

Army Form C. 2118.

Place	Date	Hour	Summary of Events and Information	Remarks and references to Appendices
Field	29/5/18		Battle continued. A party of Officers and sixty men of the Battalion proceeded to reinforce the 174th Infantry Brigade	A94/13
	30/5/18		Battle continued. Transport moved to IGNY.	P44/3
	31/5/18		Battle continued. Transport moved to AULNIZEUX.	A44/13

A.H. Bingham
Lieut Colonel
Comdg. 7th Bn. Durham Lt. Infantry

VOLUME No. 39

7TH BN THE DURHAM LIGHT INFANTRY
PIONEERS
Army Form C. 2118.

WAR DIARY
or
INTELLIGENCE SUMMARY.
(Erase heading not required.)

Place	Date	Hour	Summary of Events and Information	Remarks and references to Appendices
Field	1/6/18		Battalion continued training at ALNIZEUX 200 men in line with 50 Primary Composite Battalion	
	2/6/18		as above	
	3/6/18		as above	
	4/6/18		as above	
	5/6/18		as above	
	6/6/18		as above	
	7/6/18		as above	
	8/6/18		as above	
	9/6/18		The Battalion (less the 60 men in the line) moved to MONDEMENT.	
	10/6/18		Battalion carried out training	
	11/6/18		as above	
	12/6/18		as above	

VOLUME No 39

7TH Bn. THE DURHAM LIGHT INFANTRY
(PIONEERS)
Army Form C. 2118.

WAR DIARY
or
INTELLIGENCE SUMMARY.
(Erase heading not required.)

Instructions regarding War Diaries and Intelligence Summaries are contained in F. S. Regs., Part II. and the Staff Manual respectively. Title pages will be prepared in manuscript.

Place	Date	Hour	Summary of Events and Information	Remarks and references to Appendices
Eims	13/6/18		Battalion continued training.	
	14/6/18		as above	
	15/6/18		as above	
	16/6/18		as above	
	17/6/18		as above	
	18/6/18		as above	
	19/6/18		as above. Officers & Other ranks from 50th Division Composite Bn. rejoined unit	
	20/6/18		The Battalion transferred to the 8th Division. Battalion entrained at SEZANNE.	
	21/6/18		Battalion detrained at GAMACHES and marched to Camp at HELICOURT.	
	22/6/18		Battalion remained in camp at HELICOURT.	
	23/6/18		Battalion marched to ALLENAY and were billeted in village	

VOLUME No 39 WAR DIARY 7TH Bn. THE DURHAM Army Form C. 2118.
or
INTELLIGENCE SUMMARY. LIGHT INFANTRY
PIONEERS
(Erase heading not required.)

Place	Date	Hour	Summary of Events and Information	Remarks and references to Appendices
Tires	24/6/16		Battalion commenced training	[initials]
	25/6/16		As above	[initials]
	26/6/16		As above	[initials]
	27/6/16		As above	[initials]
	28/6/16		As above — all mobilization stores of the 22nd Bn Durham Light Infantry-Pioneers handed over to this unit.	[initials]
	29/6/16		Battalion continues training	[initials]
	30/6/16		As above.	[initials]

R.G. Price. 2/Lieut & a/Adjutant.
7/Bn. The Durham Light Infantry
Pioneers.

8th Division A

[stamp: 7th BN. DURHAM LIGHT INFANTRY PIONEERS N.129 1.7.18]

Attached herewith War Diary for the month of June 1918 in respect of this Unit.

Acknowledge

B. Chance
2/Lieut & a/Adjt
for O.C.
7th Bn. Durham L.I.
Pioneers

Went to 8th Div
20.6.18

TABLE A

First party parade in camp at:-

    Half Transport   9 AM
    'A' Coy and H.Q details 10-15 am

entrain at 4 pm.

Second party parade in camp at:-

    Half Transport   1-0 pm
    'B' & 'C' Coys   - 2-15 pm

entrain 8 pm.

Halte Repas - Montargis & Montereux.

9/6/18.

7th Bn Durham L.I. Pioneers.
Operation Order No. 142

1. The Battalion will move to MONDEMENT today.
2. The Battalion will parade in Fighting Order on the road outside Orderly Room at 7-30 am. Service dress caps to be worn.
3. Blankets in bundles of two Divs, and mess gear will be ready for collection at 6-30 am. Valises to be dumped at Q.M. Stores by 6-30 am.
4. Cpl Copland and 2 Signallers will proceed as advance party and should report to the D.A.A.G. 50th Division at the Church MONDEMENT at 7-30 am
5. A certificate to the effect that all billets have been left in a clean and sanitary condition will be rendered to Orderly Room before moving off.
6. Transport will follow in rear of Battalion.

Sgd. A H Birchall
Lt Colonel

7th Bn. Durham L. Rangers

Operation Order No 45

19/6/18

1. The Bn will move by rail from SEZANNE to the MARTAINNEVILLE area on 20th June 1918 to join the 8th Division.

2. The Battalion will parade in full marching order and in two separate parties in the camp as per Table "A" attached.

3. Officers valises, Blankets in bundles of ten and Mess Gear will be ready for collection at 10 a.m.

4. Lieut. E.A. Welsh, Cpl Coupland and L/Cpl Thornton each with bicycles will entrain with the first party and act as advance party.

5. All men will entrain with their water bottles full.

6. No man will leave the train without the permission of an Officer.

7. At each halting place the R.S.M. for first party and C.S.M. Younger for second party will detail a picquet to prevent the men from wandering too far from the train. This picquet will be responsible that there is no looting of stores during the journey.

8. The R.S.M. and C.S.M. Younger will detail 4 men from each party

to act as Regimental Police and they will report to the R.T.O. at the entraining Station four hours before departure of train.

These men should report to the R.T.O. at detraining Station immediately on arrival of their respective parties.

9. TRANSPORT.- Breast ropes for horses must be provided by the Transport Officer. Ropes for lashing vehicles will be provided by the Railway authorities. Canvas buckets will be carried in each horse truck.

Horses will be entrained saddled up. Transport men and grooms will travel in the trucks with their animals.

If possible cinders or gravel will be spread on the floor of trucks occupied by animals.

The water cart will be entrained full.

10. 2nd/Lieut Welsh will report to the entraining Officer at SEZANNE four hours before the departure of the first train with a complete marching out state of each party.

11. Rations for consumption on 22nd inst. (including ONE days Iron rations) will be carried on the trains.

12. 2/Lieut L. G. Shepherd will be in charge of the second party and will be responsible that the camp is left in a clean and sanitary condition.

13. The G.O.C. 50th Div. will inspect each party before moving out of camp.

14. Service dress caps to be worn, Steel helmets to be strapped to valise.
Waterproof sheets to be rolled around blankets.

Sgd A H Birchall
Lieut-Colonel

Issued at 8 p.m.

Issued to :-
C.O.
O.C. A Coy
- B -
- C -
T.O
Q.M
Officer i/c Details
War Diary 2
File.

www.ingramcontent.com/pod-product-compliance
Lightning Source LLC
Chambersburg PA
CBHW080904230426
43664CB00016B/2721